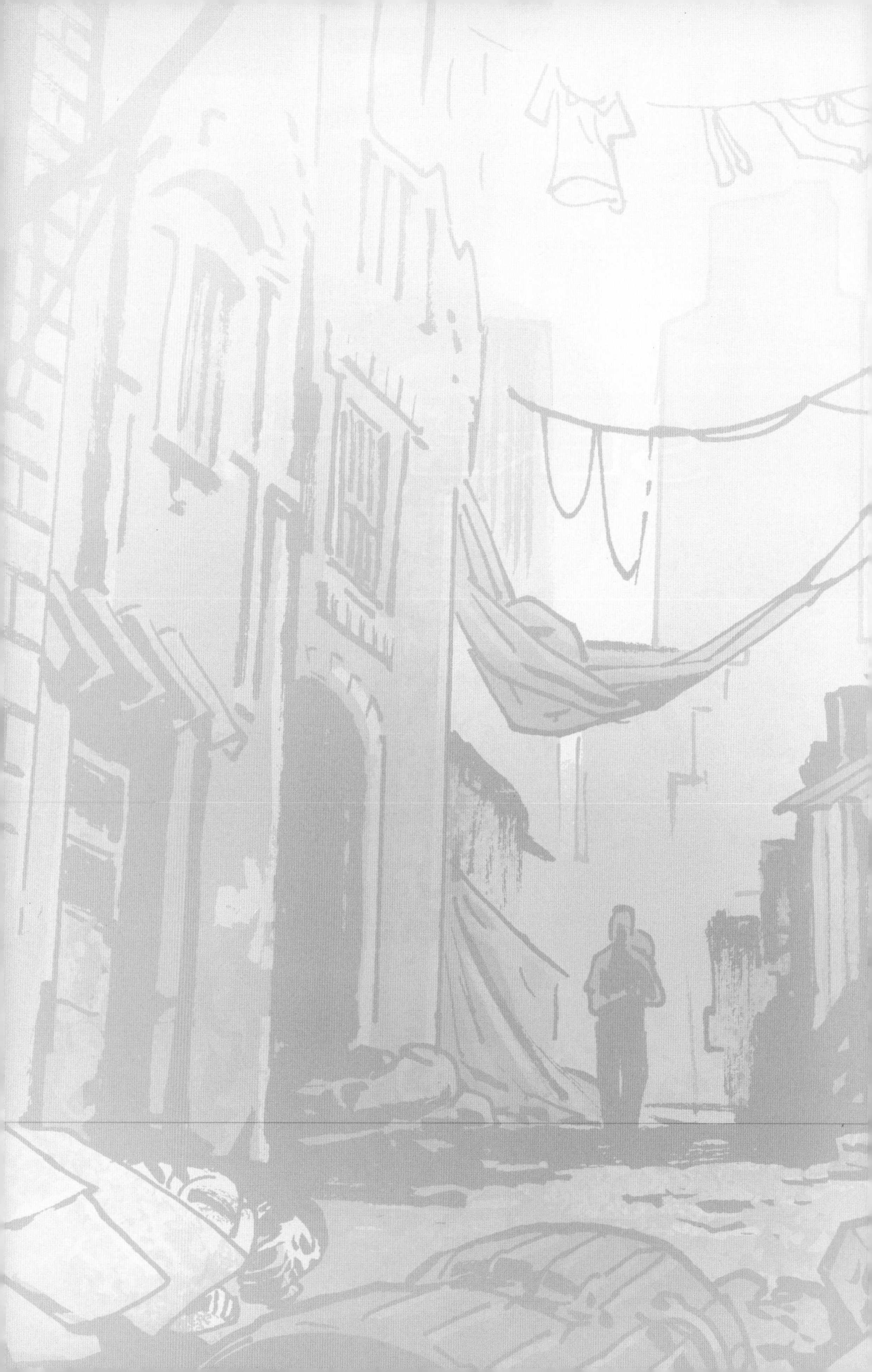

SERENITY

——— THE SHEPHERD'S TALE ———

STORY
JOSS and ZACK WHEDON

ART
CHRIS SAMNEE

COLORS
DAVE STEWART

LETTERS
MICHAEL HEISLER

COVER ART
STEVE MORRIS

DARK HORSE BOOKS®

PRESIDENT & PUBLISHER
MIKE RICHARDSON

EDITOR
SCOTT ALLIE

ASSOCIATE EDITOR
SIERRA HAHN

ASSISTANT EDITOR
FREDDYE LINS

COLLECTION DESIGNER
STEPHEN REICHERT with **DAVID NESTELLE**

SPECIAL THANKS TO CINDY CHANG AT UNIVERSAL STUDIOS AND NICKI MARON.

———————

NEIL HANKERSON Executive Vice President • TOM WEDDLE Chief Financial Officer • RANDY STRADLEY
Vice President of Publishing • MICHAEL MARTENS Vice President of Business Development • ANITA NELSON Vice
President of Business Affairs • MICHA HERSHMAN Vice President of Marketing • DAVID SCROGGY Vice President of
Product Development • DALE LAFOUNTAIN Vice President of Information Technology • DARLENE VOGEL
Director of Purchasing • KEN LIZZI General Counsel • DAVEY ESTRADA Editorial Director

A Note to Parents: *Serenity* is rated PG-13. Consult www.filmratings.com for further information.

Published by Dark Horse Books
A division of Dark Horse Comics, Inc.
10956 SE Main Street
Milwaukie, OR 97222

darkhorse.com

To find a comics shop in your area, call the Comic Shop Locator Service toll-free at (888) 266-4226.

First edition: November 2010
ISBN 978-1-59582-561-2

1 3 5 7 9 10 8 6 4 2
Printed at Midas Printing International, Ltd., Huizhou, China

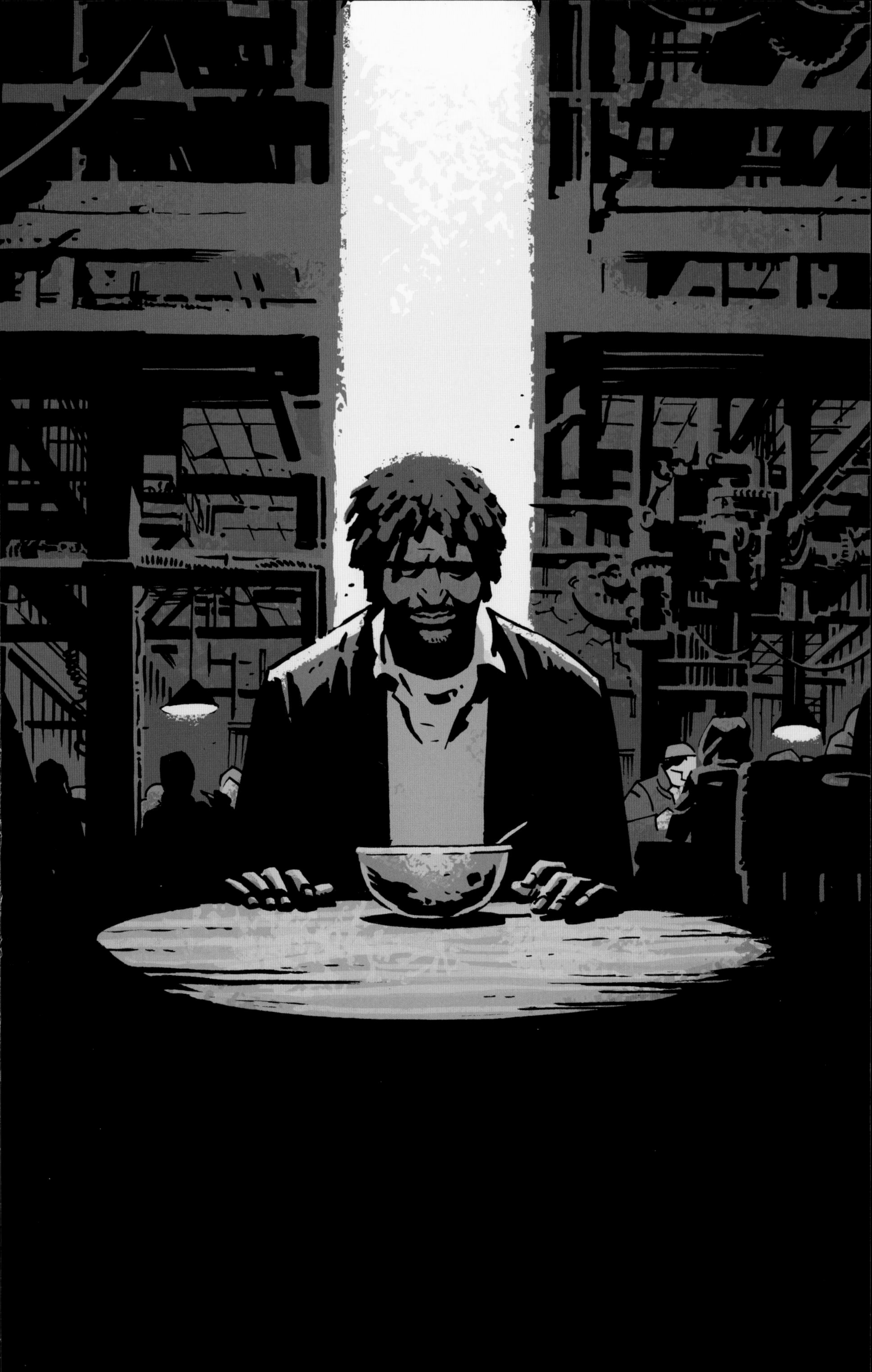

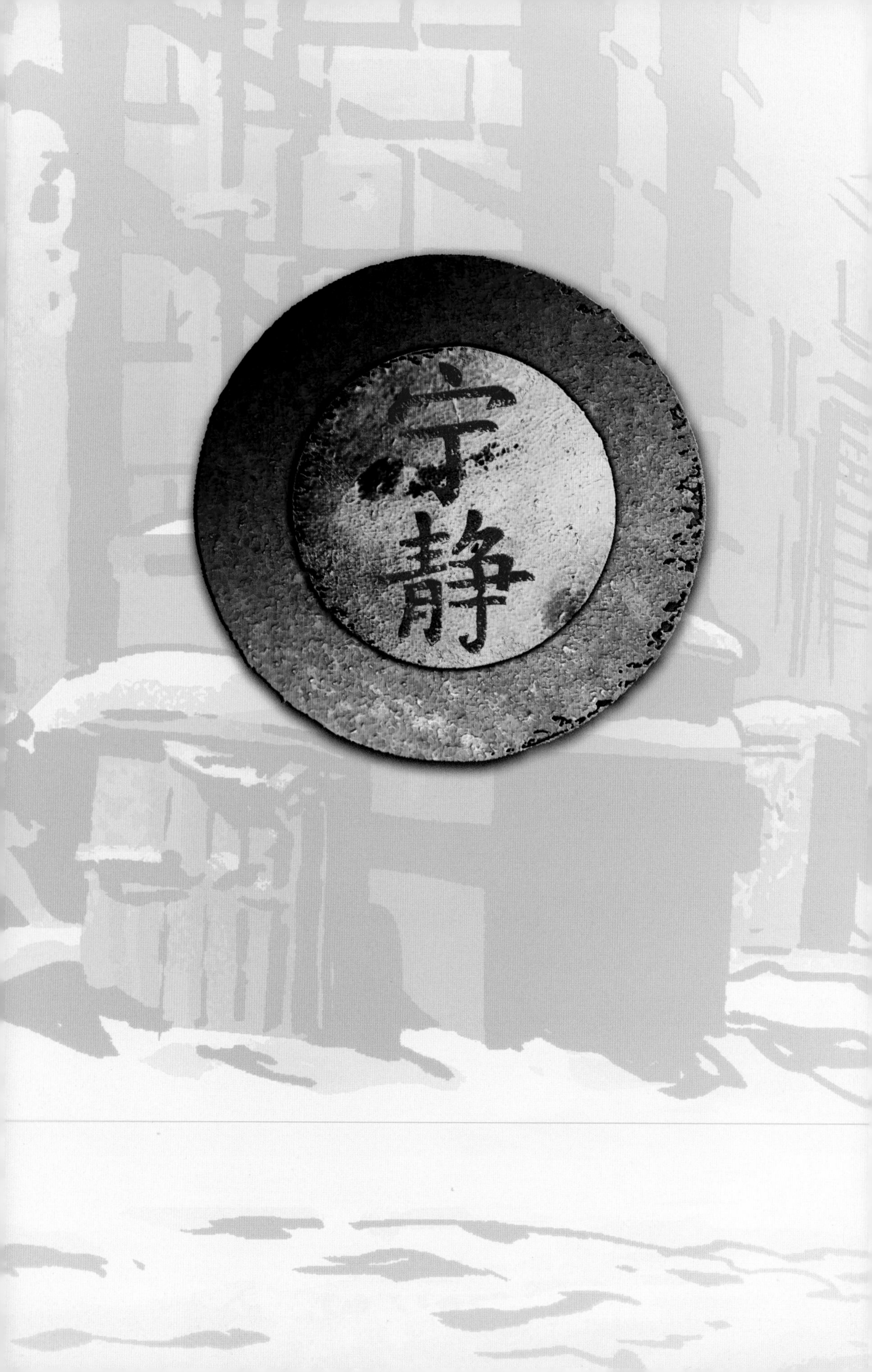
守静

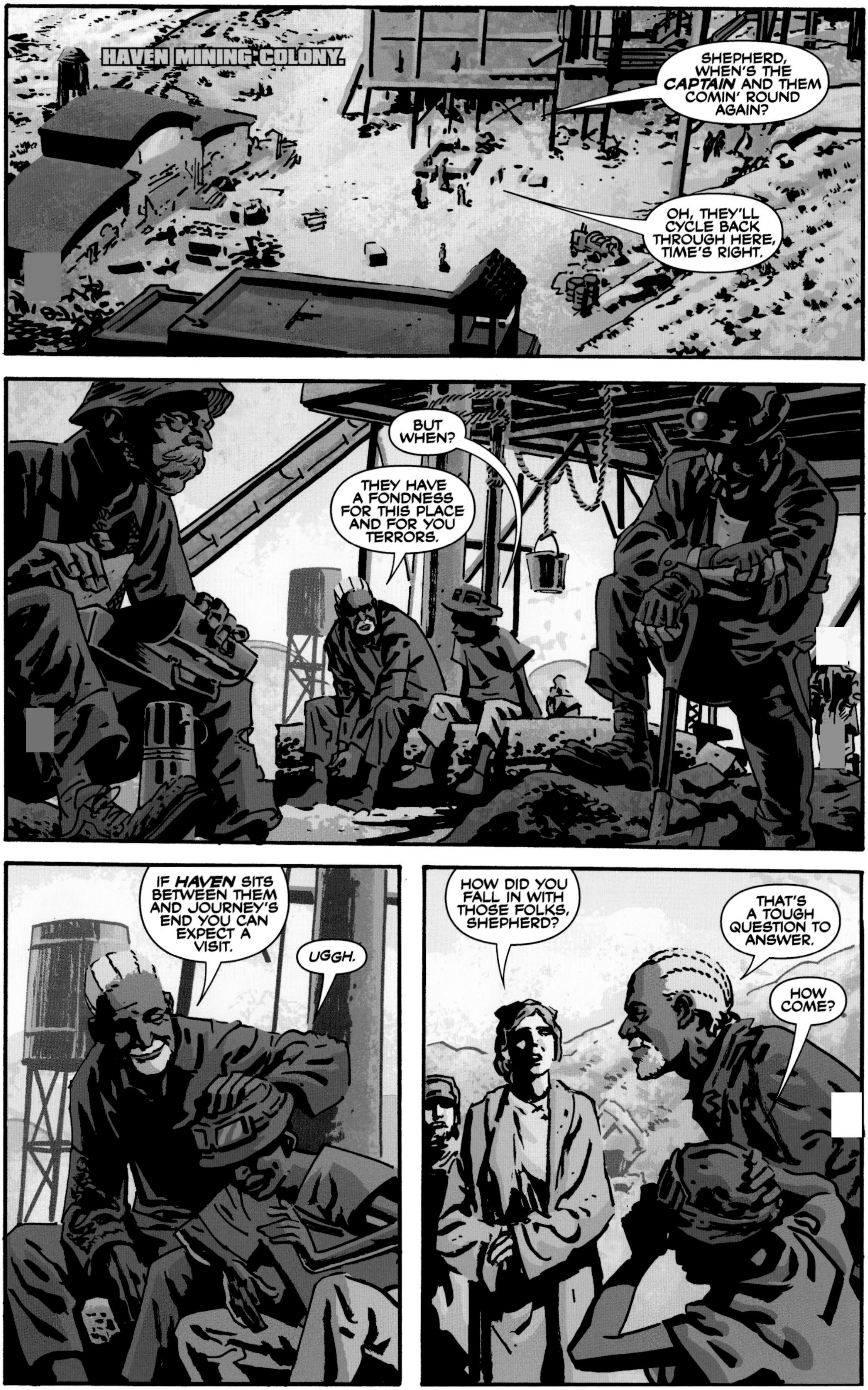
HAVEN MINING COLONY.
SHEPHERD, WHEN'S THE CAPTAIN AND THEM COMIN' ROUND AGAIN?
OH, THEY'LL CYCLE BACK THROUGH HERE, TIME'S RIGHT.
BUT WHEN?
THEY HAVE A FONDNESS FOR THIS PLACE AND FOR YOU TERRORS.
IF HAVEN SITS BETWEEN THEM AND JOURNEY'S END YOU CAN EXPECT A VISIT.
UGGH.
HOW DID YOU FALL IN WITH THOSE FOLKS, SHEPHERD?
THAT'S A TOUGH QUESTION TO ANSWER.
HOW COME?

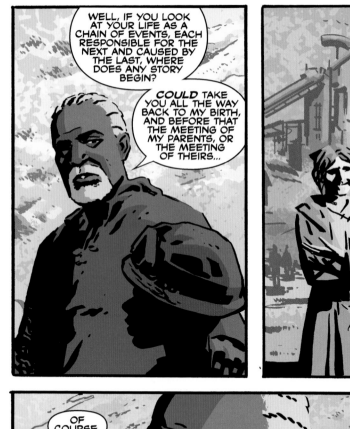

WELL, IF YOU LOOK AT YOUR LIFE AS A CHAIN OF EVENTS, EACH RESPONSIBLE FOR THE NEXT AND CAUSED BY THE LAST, WHERE DOES ANY STORY BEGIN?

COULD TAKE YOU ALL THE WAY BACK TO MY BIRTH, AND BEFORE THAT THE MEETING OF MY PARENTS, OR THE MEETING OF THEIRS...

I'M JUST ASKING HOW YOU MET THE GUY.

OF COURSE.

RUMMMMMBBBLLE

COMMERCIAL FREIGHTER. THEY COME BY HERE ALL THE TIME.

THAT'S NOT A FREIGHTER.

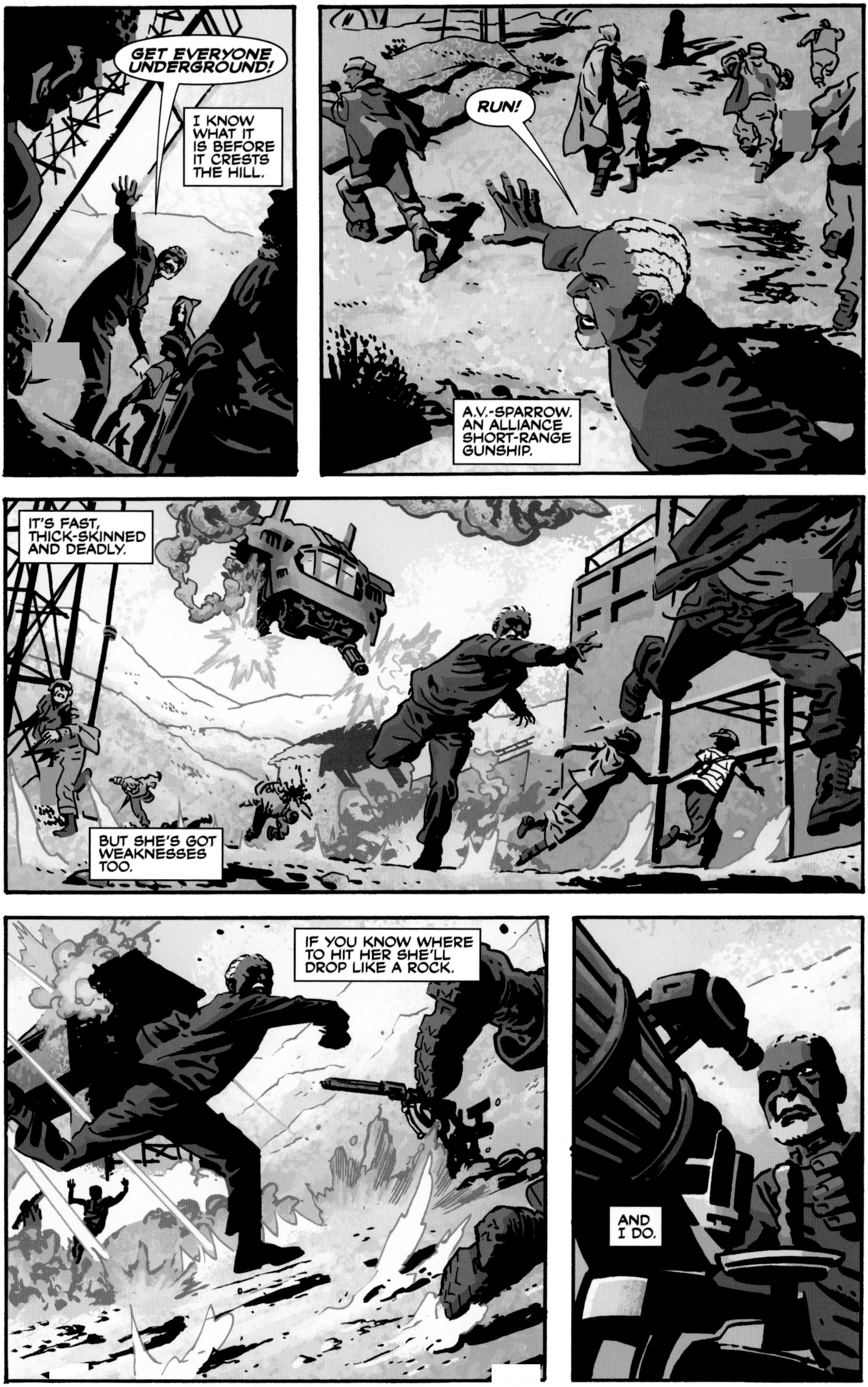
GET EVERYONE UNDERGROUND!
I KNOW WHAT IT IS BEFORE IT CRESTS THE HILL.
RUN!
A.V.-SPARROW. AN ALLIANCE SHORT-RANGE GUNSHIP.
IT'S FAST, THICK-SKINNED AND DEADLY.
BUT SHE'S GOT WEAKNESSES TOO.
IF YOU KNOW WHERE TO HIT HER SHE'LL DROP LIKE A ROCK.
AND I DO.

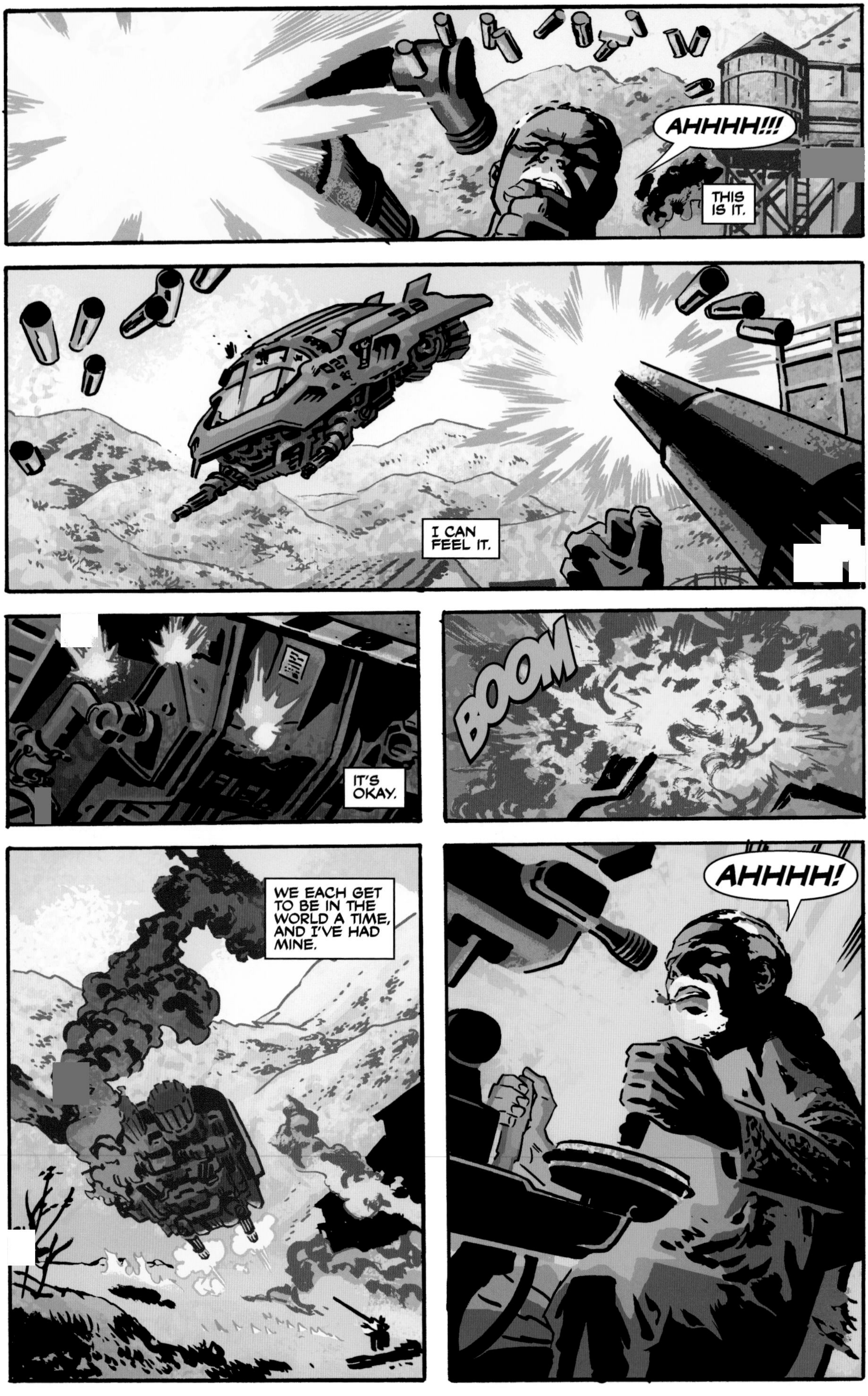
AHHHH!!!
THIS IS IT.
I CAN FEEL IT.
IT'S OKAY.
BOOM
WE EACH GET TO BE IN THE WORLD A TIME, AND I'VE HAD MINE.
AHHHH!

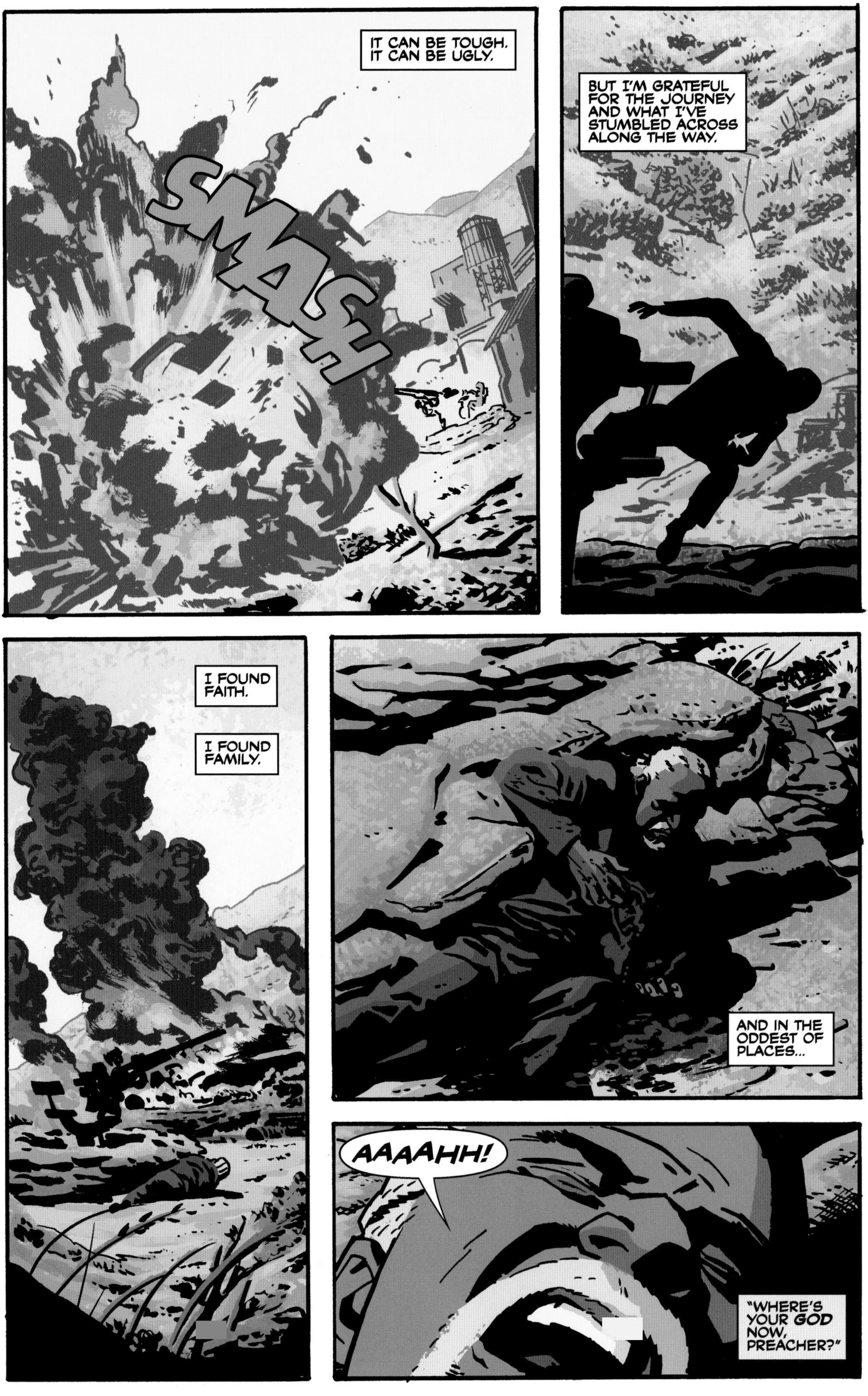
IT CAN BE TOUGH, IT CAN BE UGLY.
SMASH
BUT I'M GRATEFUL FOR THE JOURNEY AND WHAT I'VE STUMBLED ACROSS ALONG THE WAY.
I FOUND FAITH.
I FOUND FAMILY.
AND IN THE ODDEST OF PLACES...
AAAAHH!
"WHERE'S YOUR GOD NOW, PREACHER?"

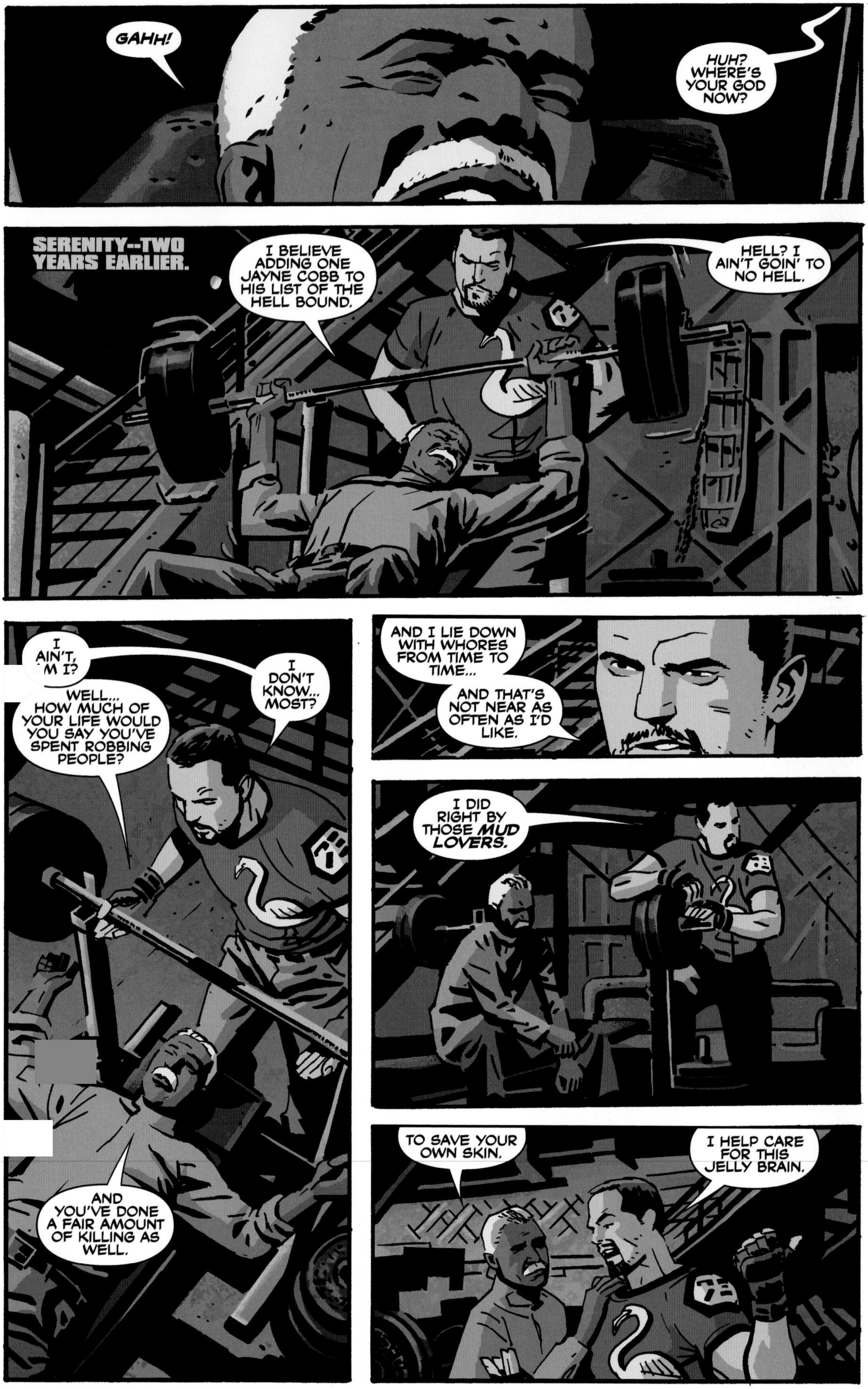

GAHH!
HUH? WHERE'S YOUR GOD NOW?
SERENITY--TWO YEARS EARLIER.
I BELIEVE ADDING ONE JAYNE COBB TO HIS LIST OF THE HELL BOUND.
HELL? I AIN'T GOIN' TO NO HELL.
I AIN'T, M I?
I DON'T KNOW... MOST?
WELL... HOW MUCH OF YOUR LIFE WOULD YOU SAY YOU'VE SPENT ROBBING PEOPLE?
AND YOU'VE DONE A FAIR AMOUNT OF KILLING AS WELL.
AND I LIE DOWN WITH WHORES FROM TIME TO TIME...
AND THAT'S NOT NEAR AS OFTEN AS I'D LIKE.
I DID RIGHT BY THOSE *MUD LOVERS.*
TO SAVE YOUR OWN SKIN.
I HELP CARE FOR THIS JELLY BRAIN.

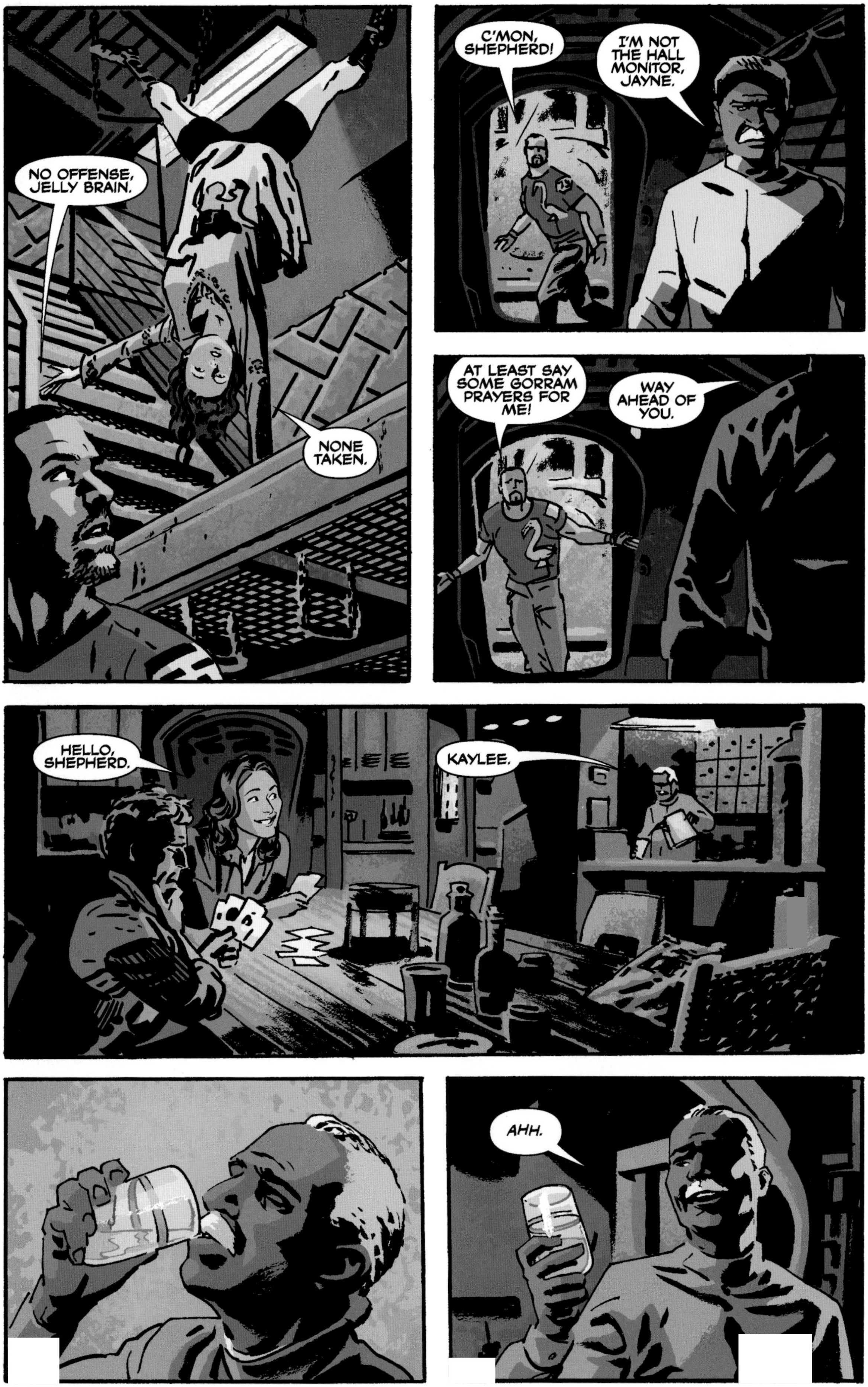
NO OFFENSE, JELLY BRAIN.
NONE TAKEN.
C'MON, SHEPHERD!
I'M NOT THE HALL MONITOR, JAYNE.
AT LEAST SAY SOME GORRAM PRAYERS FOR ME!
WAY AHEAD OF YOU.
HELLO, SHEPHERD.
KAYLEE.
AHH.

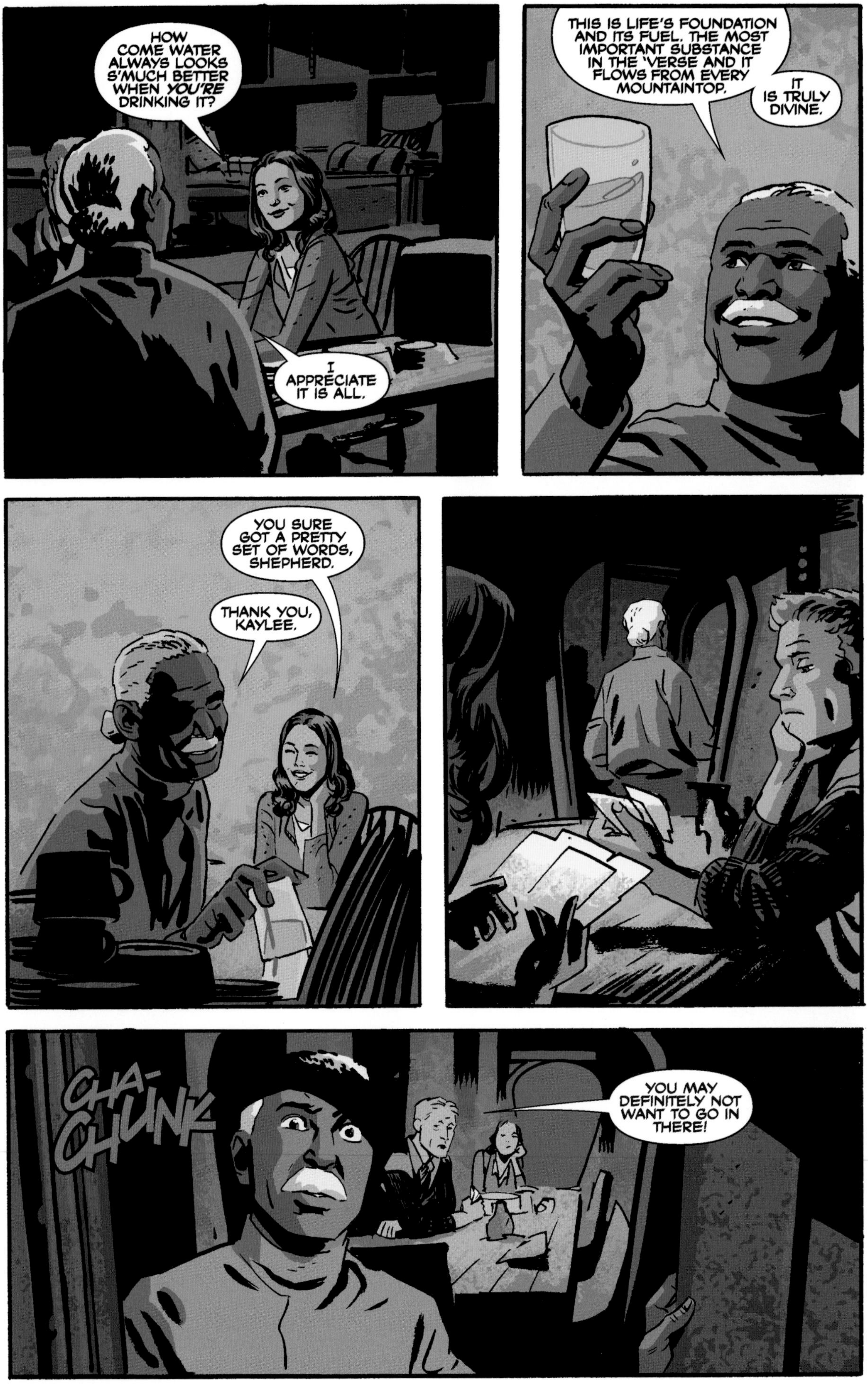
HOW COME WATER ALWAYS LOOKS S'MUCH BETTER WHEN *YOU'RE* DRINKING IT?
I APPRECIATE IT IS ALL.
THIS IS LIFE'S FOUNDATION AND ITS FUEL. THE MOST IMPORTANT SUBSTANCE IN THE 'VERSE AND IT FLOWS FROM EVERY MOUNTAINTOP.
IT IS TRULY DIVINE.
YOU SURE GOT A PRETTY SET OF WORDS, SHEPHERD.
THANK YOU, KAYLEE.
CHA-CHUNK
YOU MAY DEFINITELY NOT WANT TO GO IN THERE!

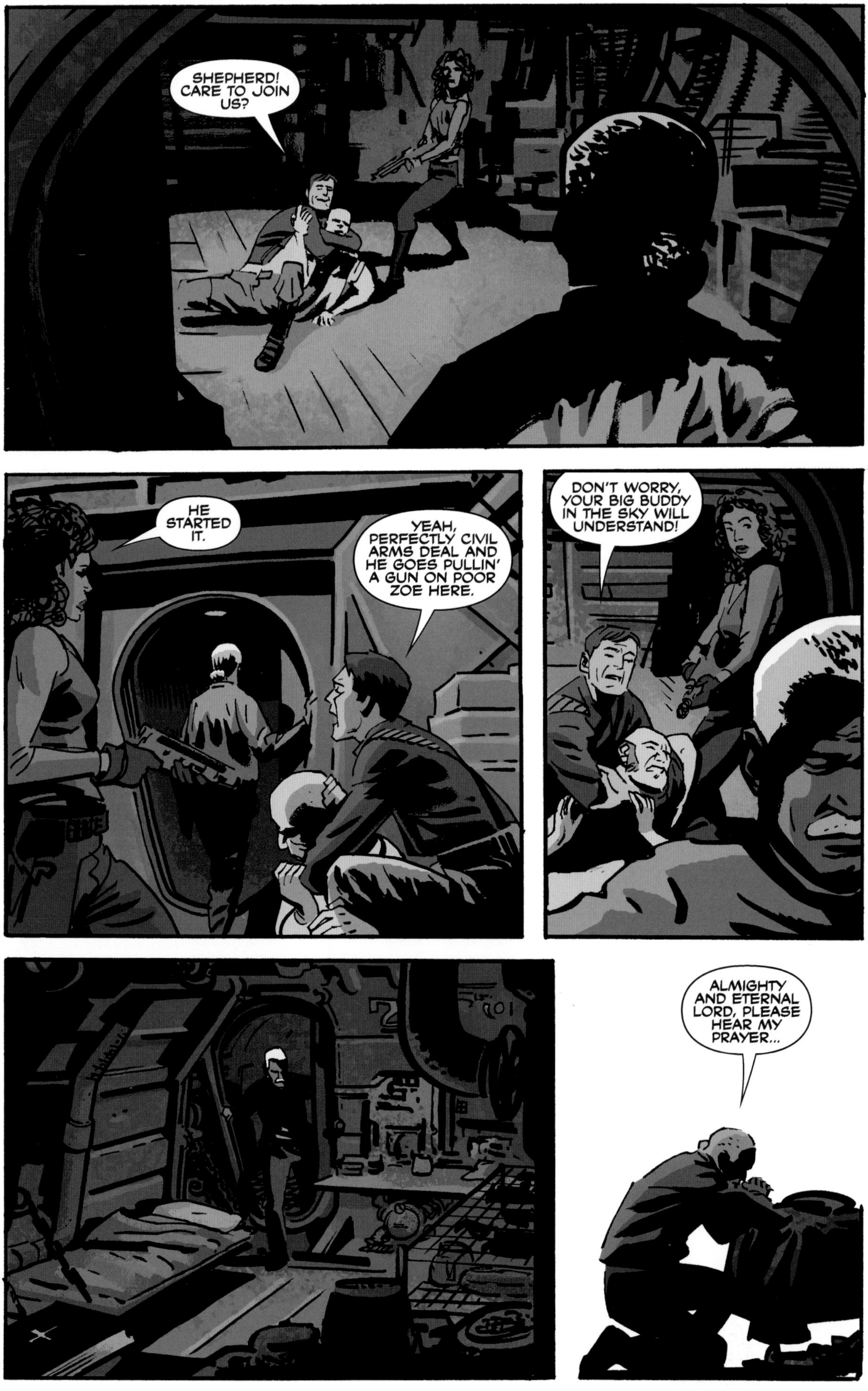
SHEPHERD! CARE TO JOIN US?
HE STARTED IT.
YEAH, PERFECTLY CIVIL ARMS DEAL AND HE GOES PULLIN' A GUN ON POOR ZOE HERE.
DON'T WORRY, YOUR BIG BUDDY IN THE SKY WILL UNDERSTAND!
ALMIGHTY AND ETERNAL LORD, PLEASE HEAR MY PRAYER...

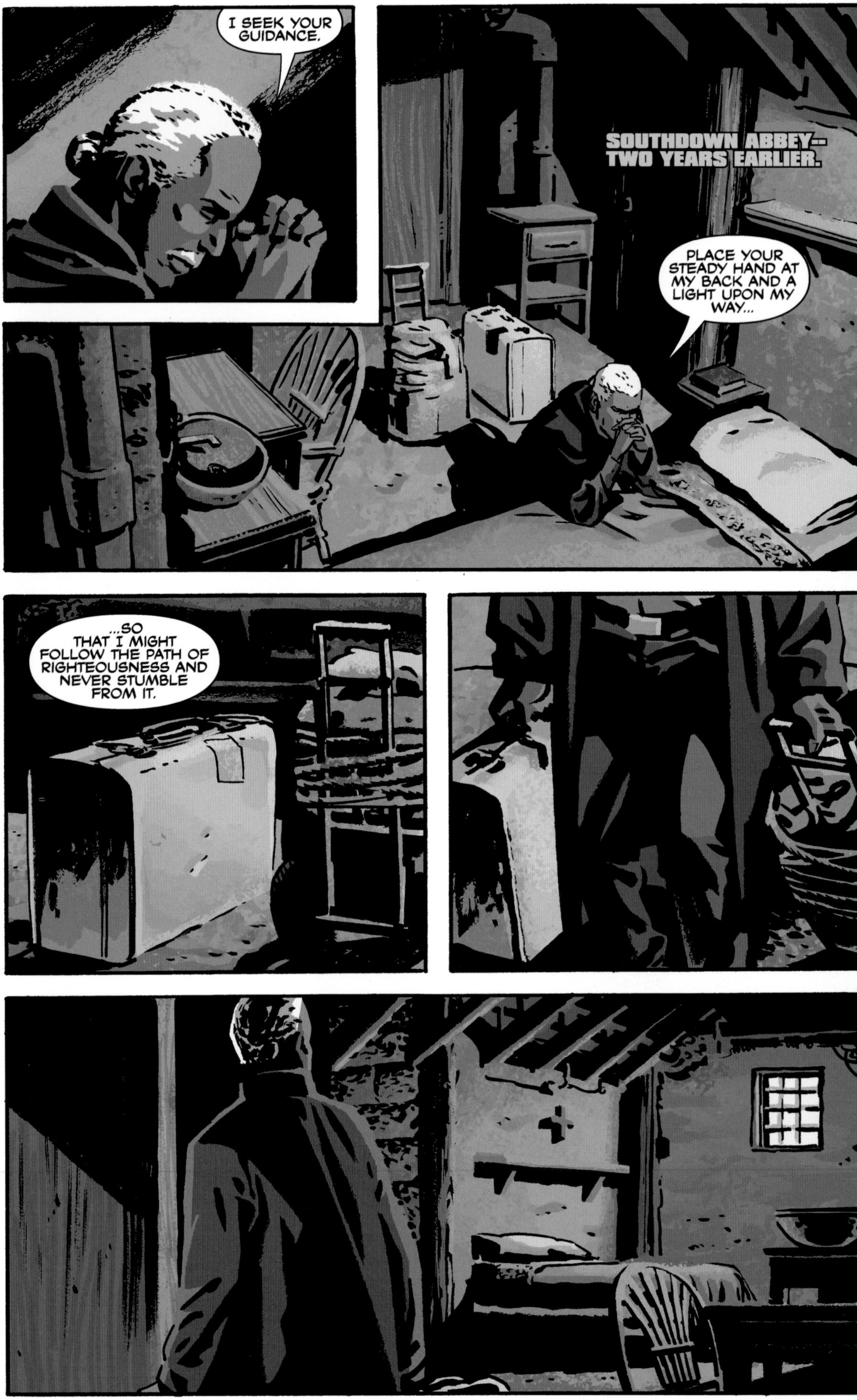
I SEEK YOUR GUIDANCE.
SOUTHDOWN ABBEY-- TWO YEARS EARLIER.
PLACE YOUR STEADY HAND AT MY BACK AND A LIGHT UPON MY WAY...
...SO THAT I MIGHT FOLLOW THE PATH OF RIGHTEOUSNESS AND NEVER STUMBLE FROM IT.

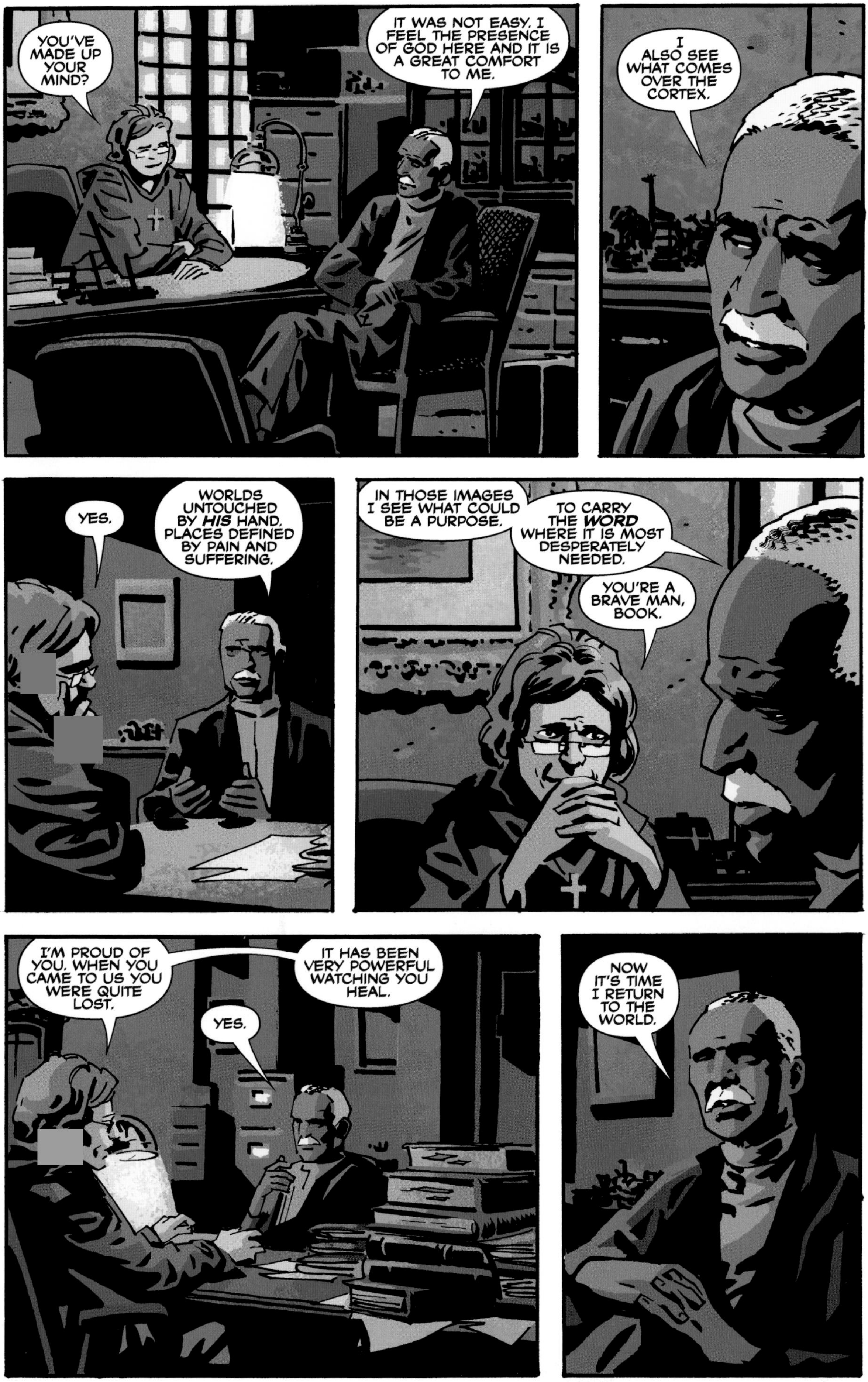
YOU'VE MADE UP YOUR MIND?
IT WAS NOT EASY. I FEEL THE PRESENCE OF GOD HERE AND IT IS A GREAT COMFORT TO ME.
I ALSO SEE WHAT COMES OVER THE CORTEX.
YES.
WORLDS UNTOUCHED BY ***HIS*** HAND. PLACES DEFINED BY PAIN AND SUFFERING.
IN THOSE IMAGES I SEE WHAT COULD BE A PURPOSE.
TO CARRY THE ***WORD*** WHERE IT IS MOST DESPERATELY NEEDED.
YOU'RE A BRAVE MAN, BOOK.
I'M PROUD OF YOU. WHEN YOU CAME TO US YOU WERE QUITE LOST.
IT HAS BEEN VERY POWERFUL WATCHING YOU HEAL.
YES.
NOW IT'S TIME I RETURN TO THE WORLD.

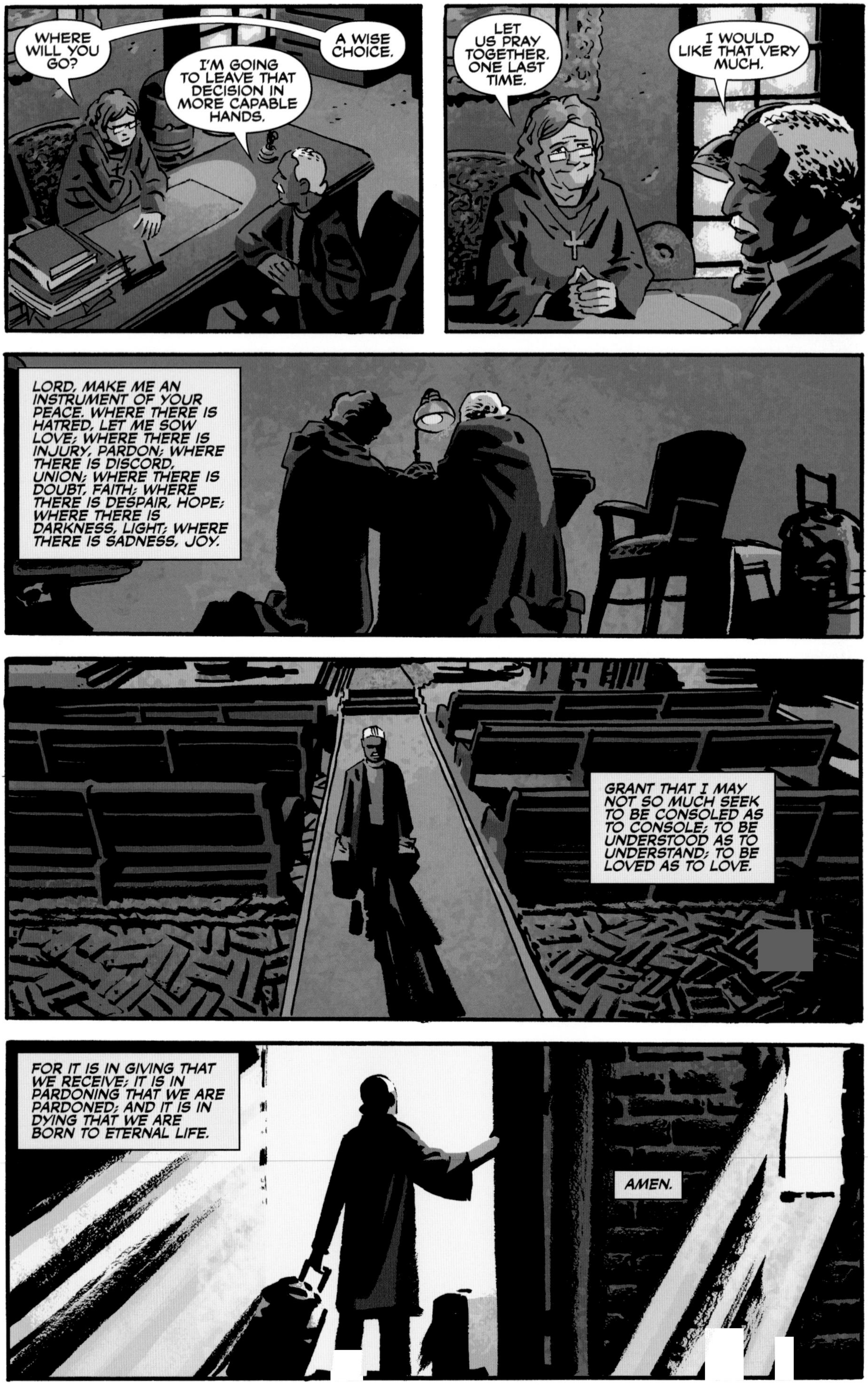
WHERE WILL YOU GO?
I'M GOING TO LEAVE THAT DECISION IN MORE CAPABLE HANDS.
A WISE CHOICE.
LET US PRAY TOGETHER. ONE LAST TIME.
I WOULD LIKE THAT VERY MUCH.
LORD, MAKE ME AN INSTRUMENT OF YOUR PEACE. WHERE THERE IS HATRED, LET ME SOW LOVE; WHERE THERE IS INJURY, PARDON; WHERE THERE IS DISCORD, UNION; WHERE THERE IS DOUBT, FAITH; WHERE THERE IS DESPAIR, HOPE; WHERE THERE IS DARKNESS, LIGHT; WHERE THERE IS SADNESS, JOY.
GRANT THAT I MAY NOT SO MUCH SEEK TO BE CONSOLED AS TO CONSOLE; TO BE UNDERSTOOD AS TO UNDERSTAND; TO BE LOVED AS TO LOVE.
FOR IT IS IN GIVING THAT WE RECEIVE; IT IS IN PARDONING THAT WE ARE PARDONED; AND IT IS IN DYING THAT WE ARE BORN TO ETERNAL LIFE.
AMEN.

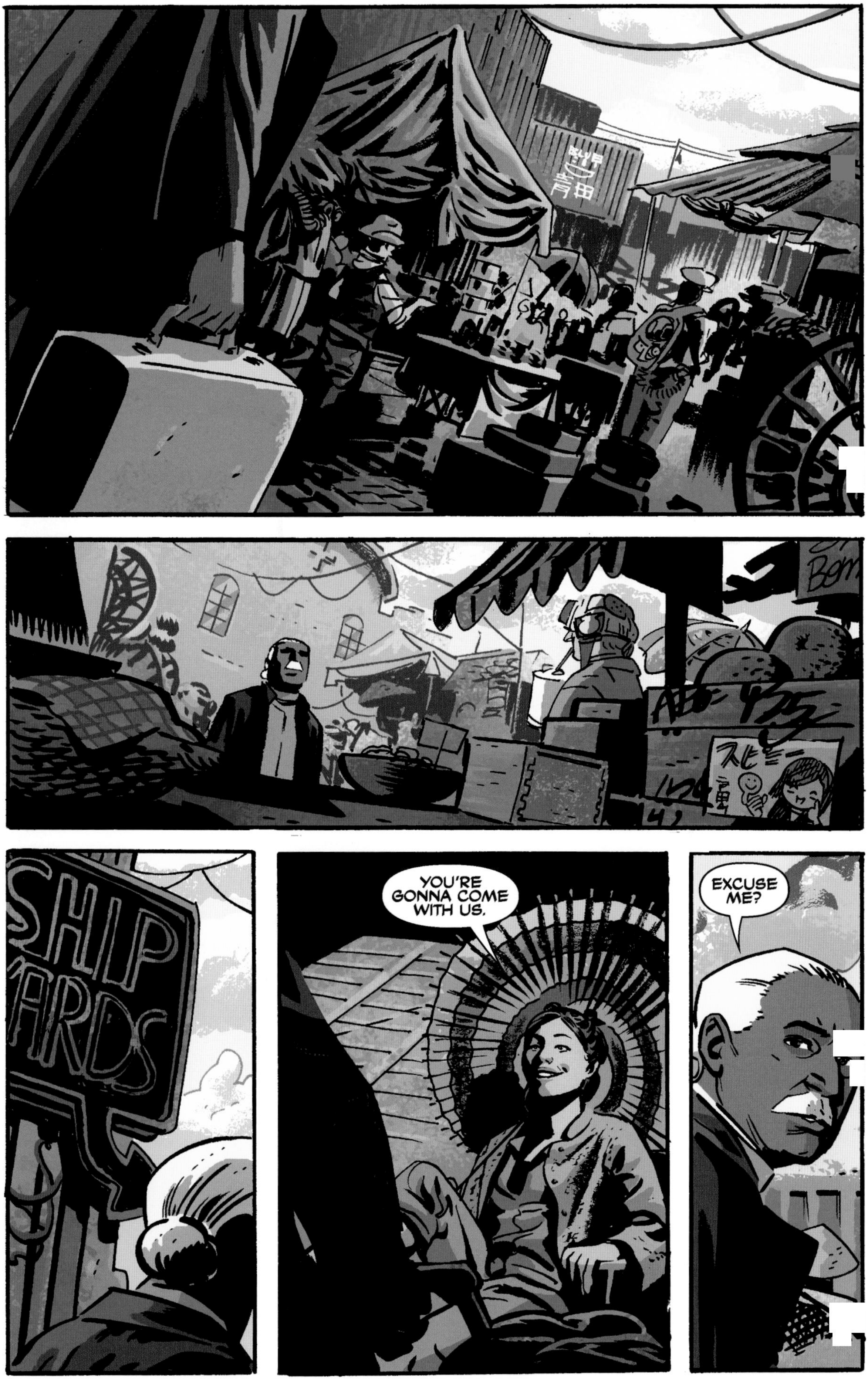
SHIP
ARDS
YOU'RE GONNA COME WITH US.
EXCUSE ME?

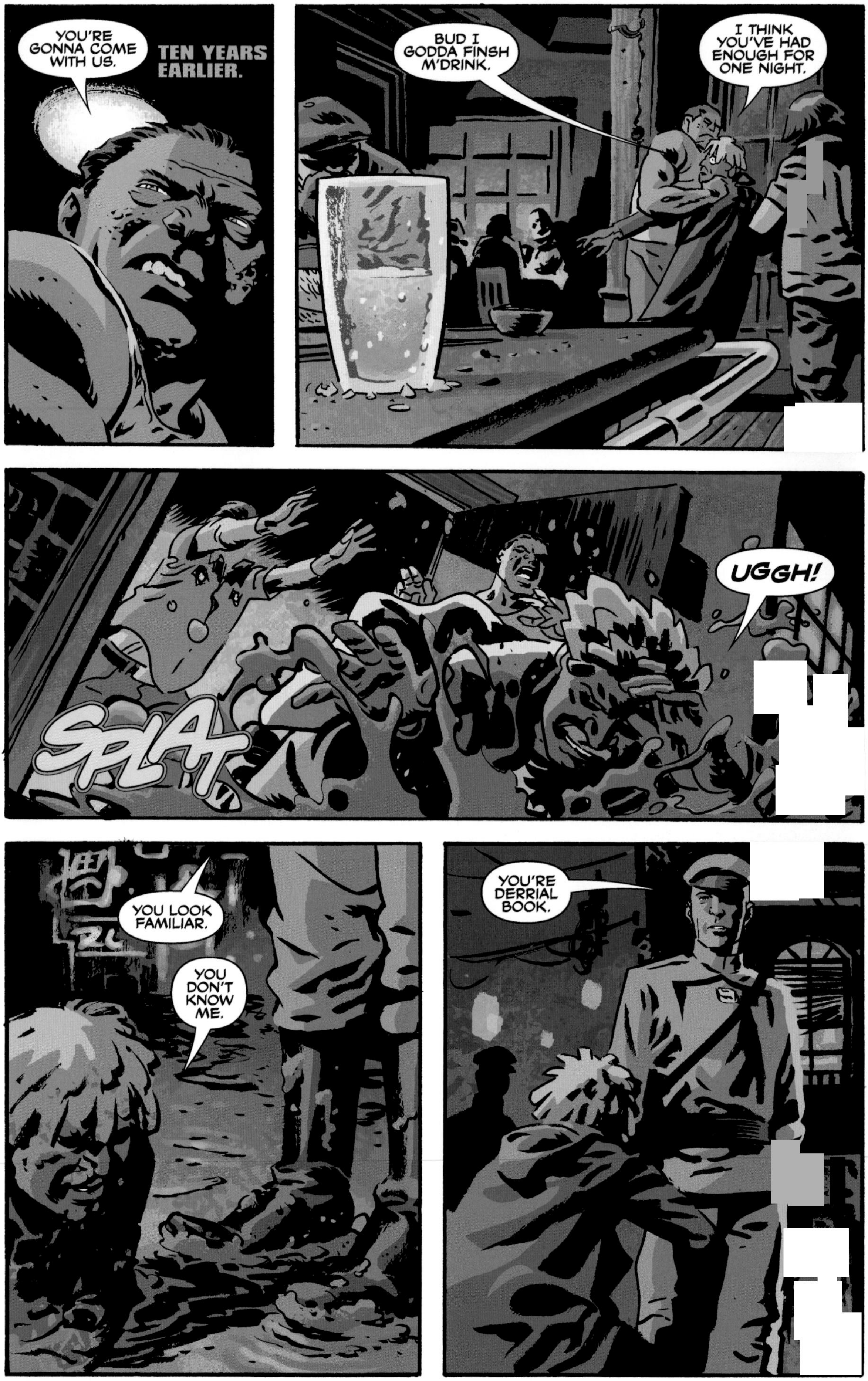
YOU'RE GONNA COME WITH US.
TEN YEARS EARLIER.
BUD I GODDA FINSH M'DRINK.
I THINK YOU'VE HAD ENOUGH FOR ONE NIGHT.
UGGH!
SPLAT
YOU LOOK FAMILIAR.
YOU DON'T KNOW ME.
YOU'RE DERRIAL BOOK.

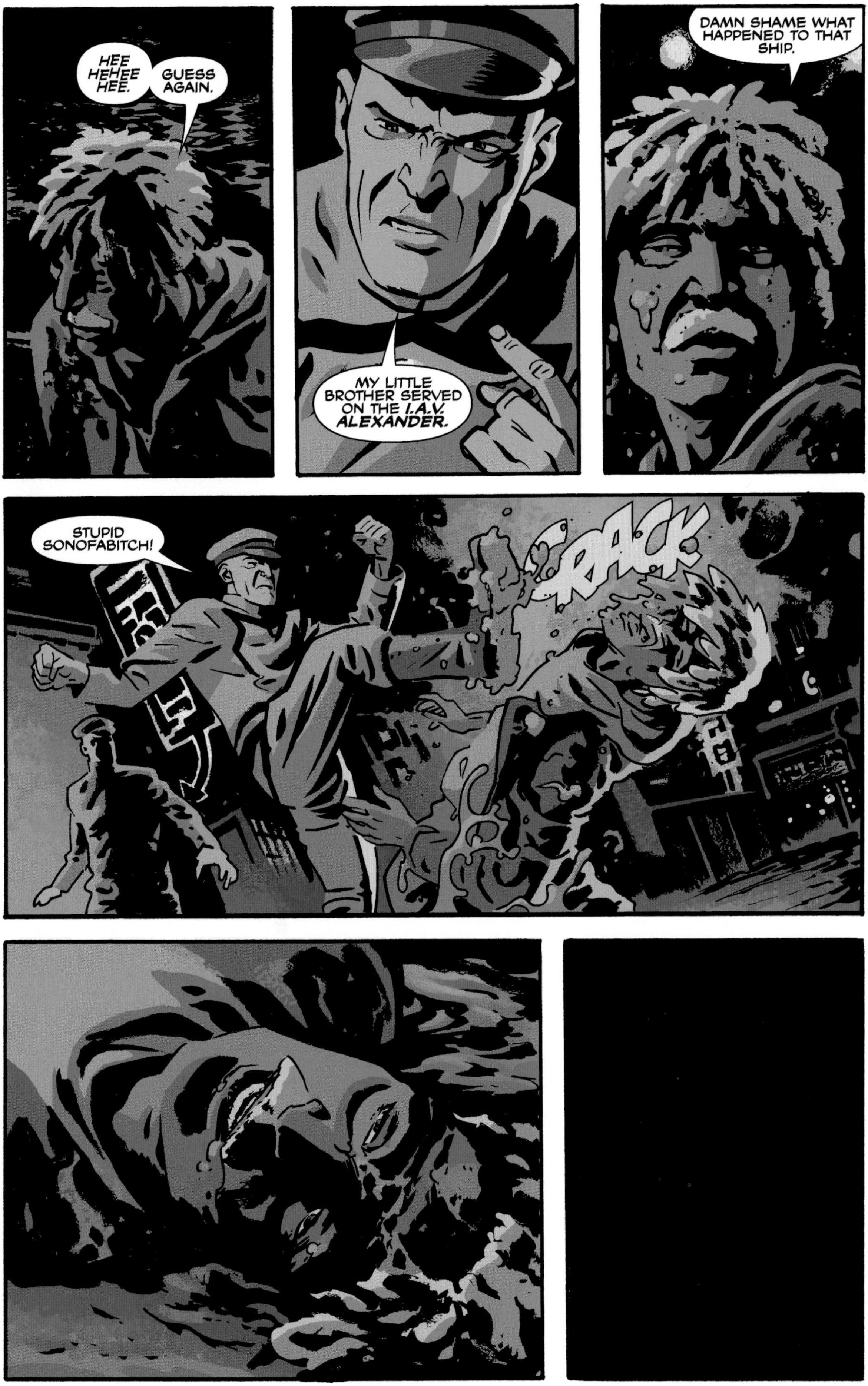
HEE HEHEE HEE.
GUESS AGAIN.
MY LITTLE BROTHER SERVED ON THE *I.A.V. ALEXANDER.*
DAMN SHAME WHAT HAPPENED TO THAT SHIP.
STUPID SONOFABITCH!
CRACK

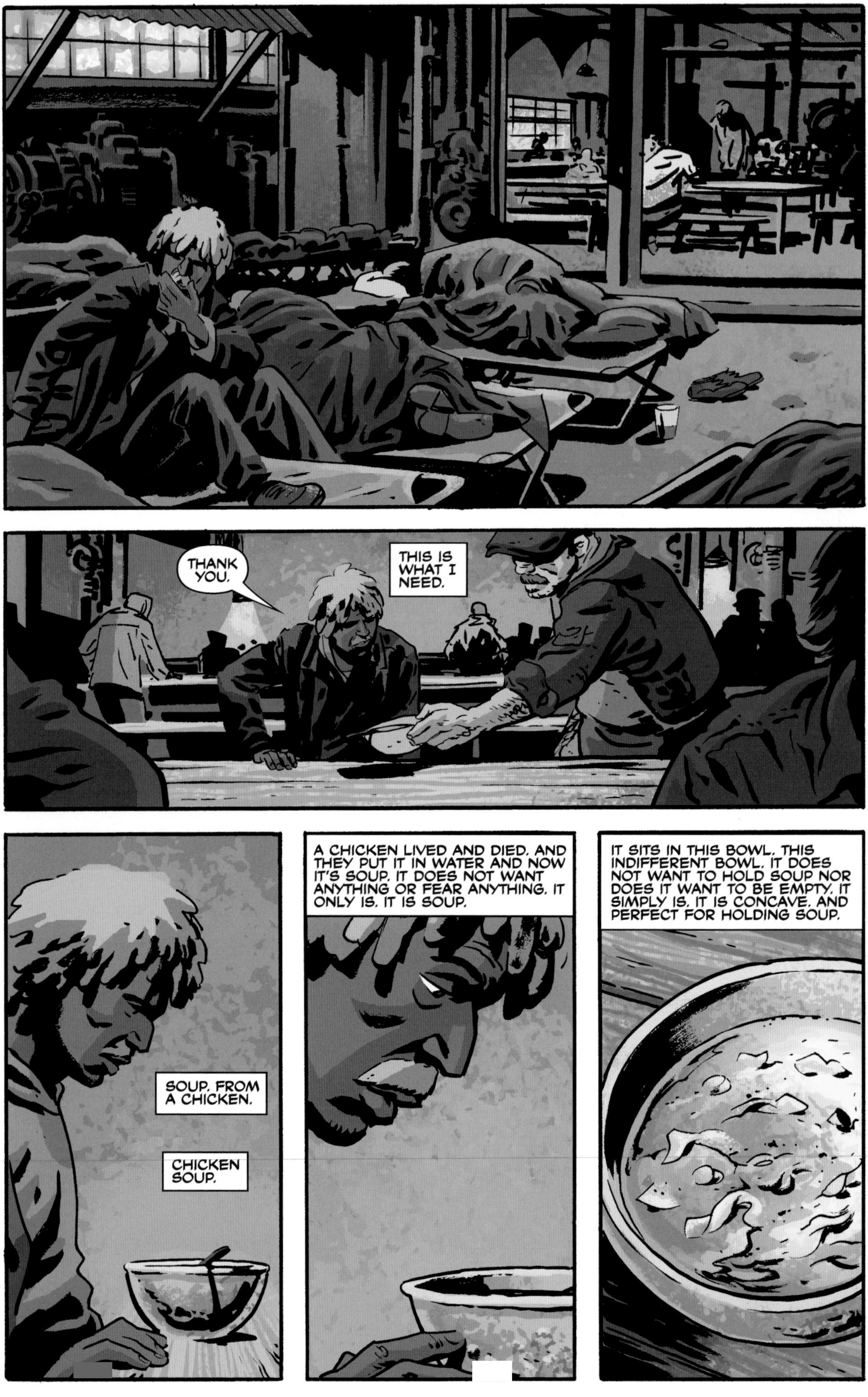
THANK YOU.
THIS IS WHAT I NEED.
SOUP. FROM A CHICKEN.
CHICKEN SOUP.
A CHICKEN LIVED AND DIED. AND THEY PUT IT IN WATER AND NOW IT'S SOUP. IT DOES NOT WANT ANYTHING OR FEAR ANYTHING. IT ONLY IS. IT IS SOUP.
IT SITS IN THIS BOWL. THIS INDIFFERENT BOWL. IT DOES NOT WANT TO HOLD SOUP NOR DOES IT WANT TO BE EMPTY. IT SIMPLY IS. IT IS CONCAVE. AND PERFECT FOR HOLDING SOUP.

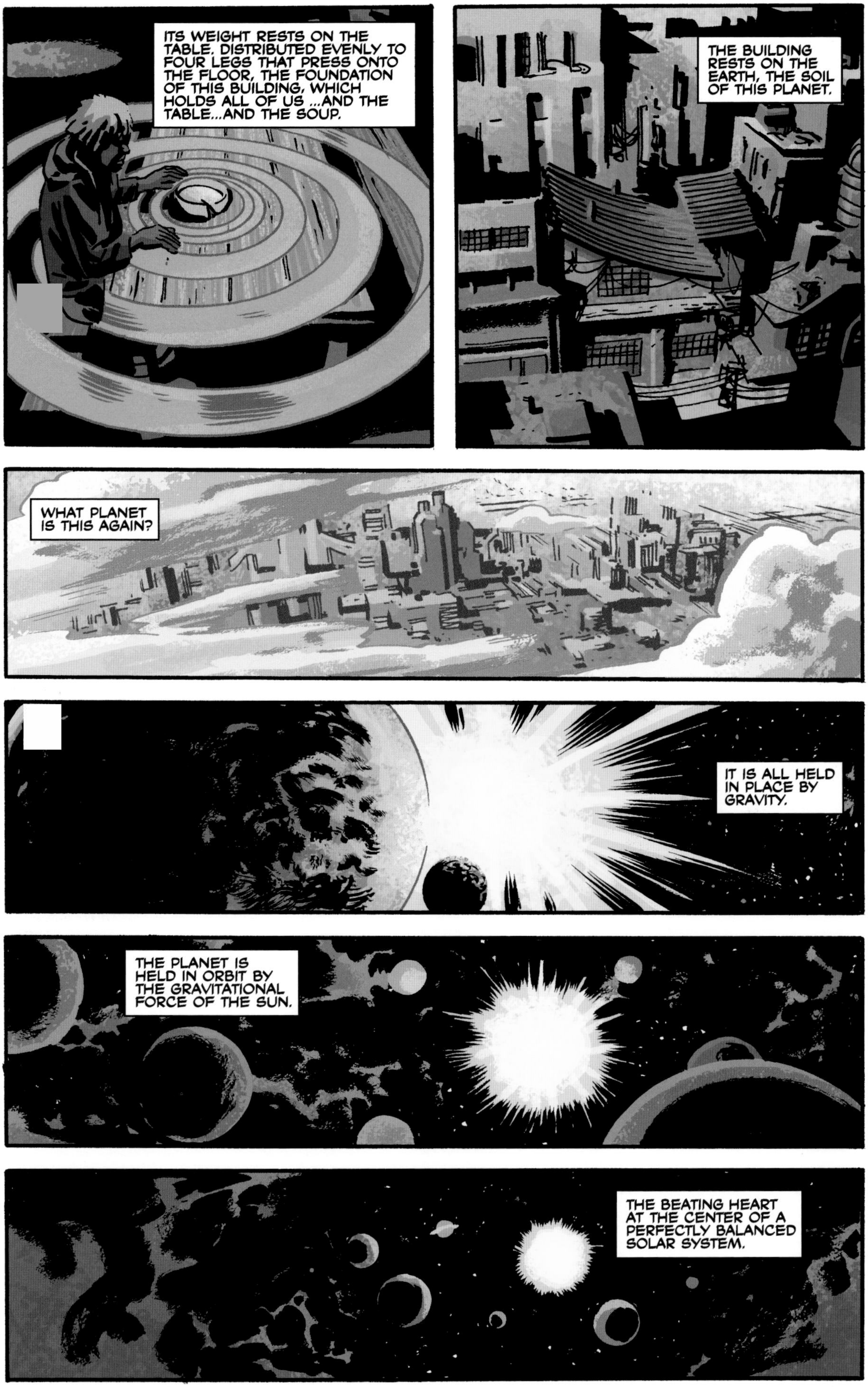
ITS WEIGHT RESTS ON THE TABLE. DISTRIBUTED EVENLY TO FOUR LEGS THAT PRESS ONTO THE FLOOR, THE FOUNDATION OF THIS BUILDING, WHICH HOLDS ALL OF US ...AND THE TABLE...AND THE SOUP.
THE BUILDING RESTS ON THE EARTH, THE SOIL OF THIS PLANET.
WHAT PLANET IS THIS AGAIN?
IT IS ALL HELD IN PLACE BY GRAVITY.
THE PLANET IS HELD IN ORBIT BY THE GRAVITATIONAL FORCE OF THE SUN.
THE BEATING HEART AT THE CENTER OF A PERFECTLY BALANCED SOLAR SYSTEM.

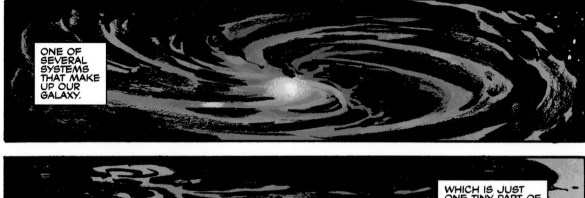

ONE OF SEVERAL SYSTEMS THAT MAKE UP OUR GALAXY.

WHICH IS JUST ONE TINY PART OF AN UNIMAGINABLE COSMIC EXPANSE.

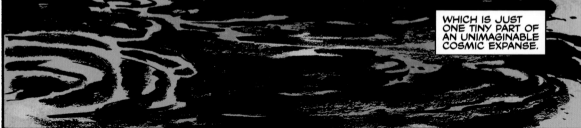

THE UNIVERSE.

EXISTENCE.

ALL OF CREATION SUPPORTS THIS BOWL.

WHICH SUPPORTS THE SOUP. WHICH SUPPORTS ME.

IT GIVES ME LIFE.

WHAT DO I DO WITH THE LIFE IT GIVES ME?

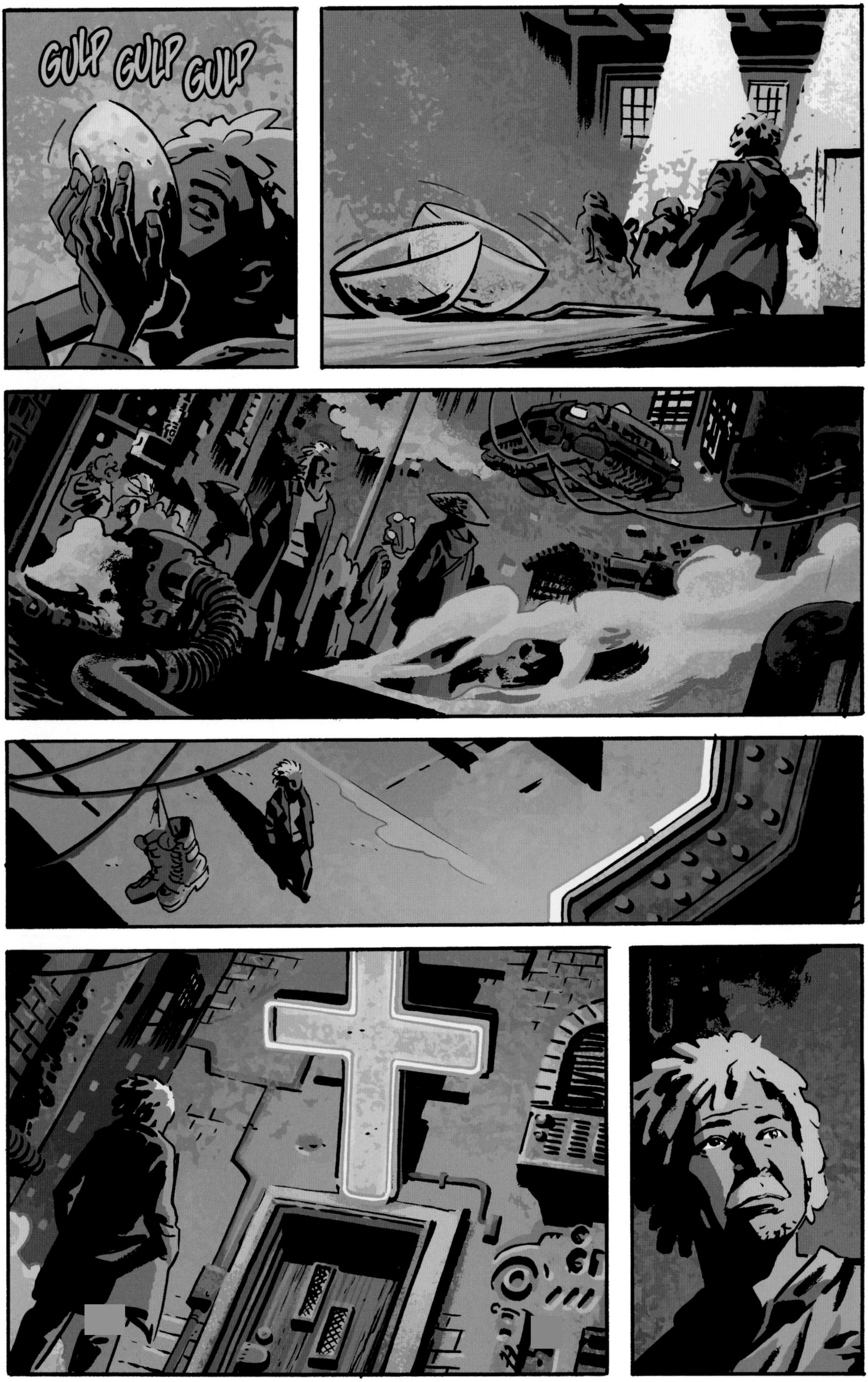
GULP GULP GULP

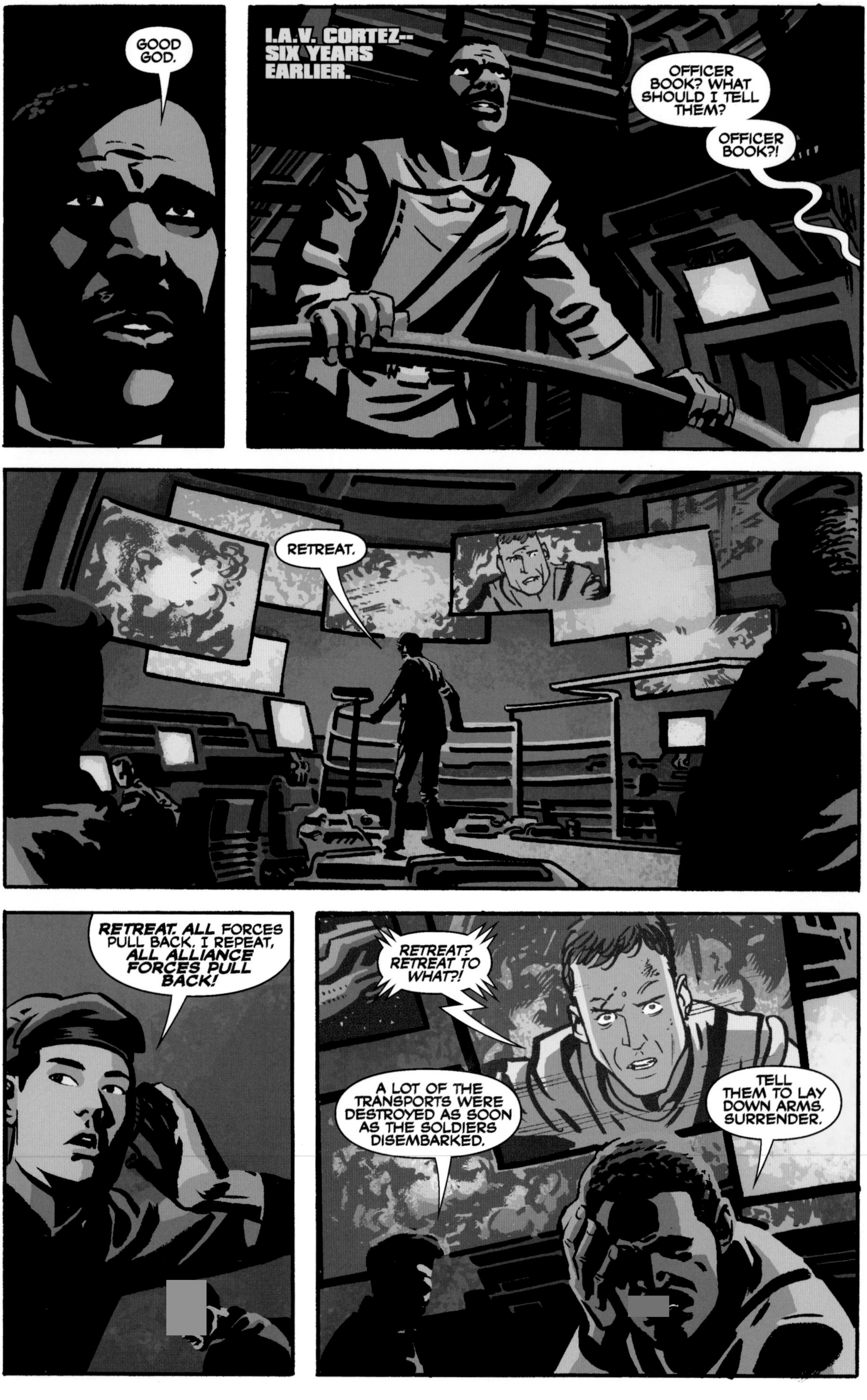
GOOD GOD.
I.A.V. CORTEZ-- SIX YEARS EARLIER.
OFFICER BOOK? WHAT SHOULD I TELL THEM?
OFFICER BOOK?!
RETREAT.
RETREAT. ALL FORCES PULL BACK. I REPEAT, ALL ALLIANCE FORCES PULL BACK!
RETREAT? RETREAT TO WHAT?!
A LOT OF THE TRANSPORTS WERE DESTROYED AS SOON AS THE SOLDIERS DISEMBARKED.
TELL THEM TO LAY DOWN ARMS. SURRENDER.

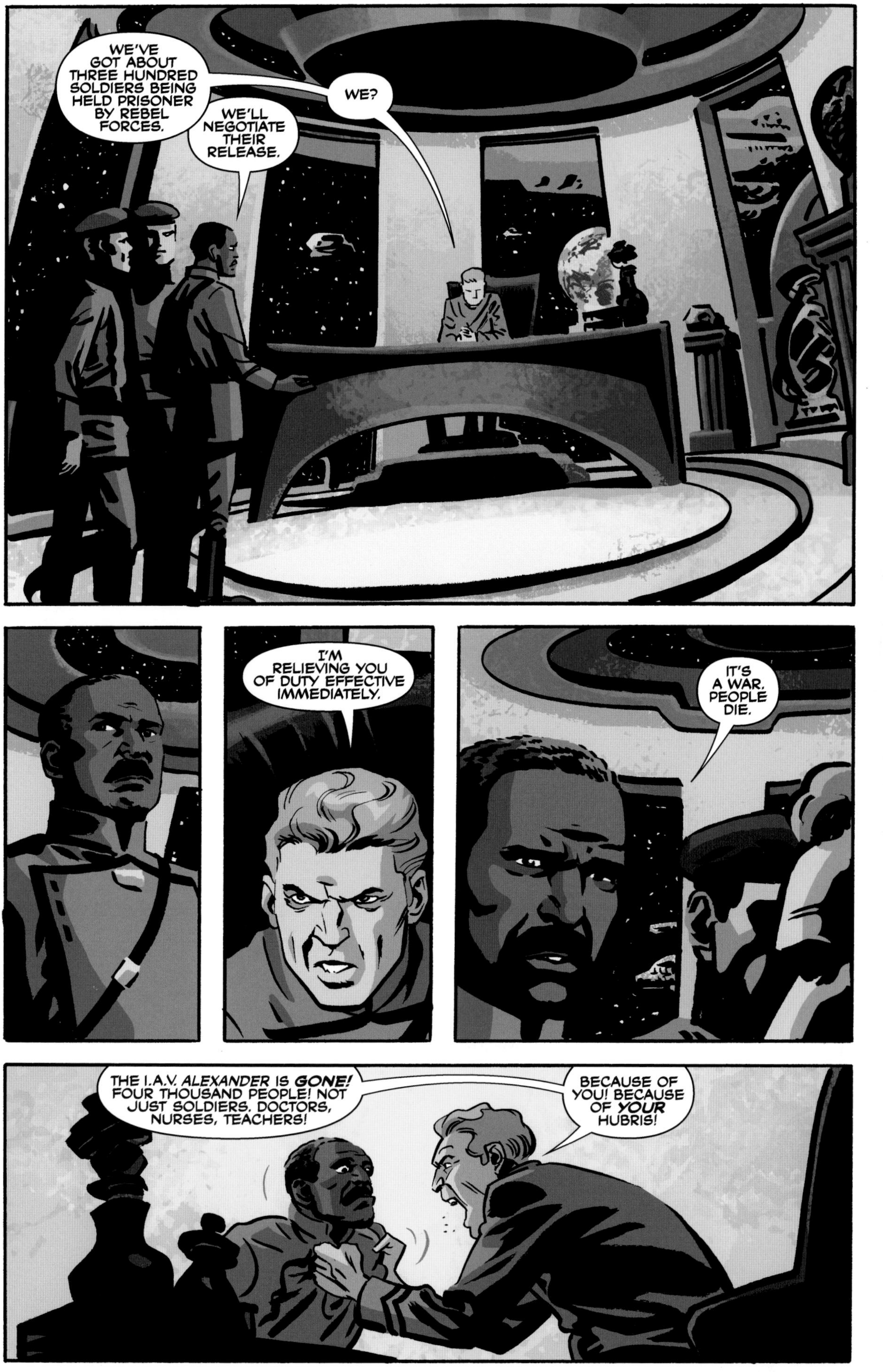
WE'VE GOT ABOUT THREE HUNDRED SOLDIERS BEING HELD PRISONER BY REBEL FORCES.
WE'LL NEGOTIATE THEIR RELEASE.
WE?
I'M RELIEVING YOU OF DUTY EFFECTIVE IMMEDIATELY.
IT'S A WAR. PEOPLE DIE.
THE I.A.V. *ALEXANDER* IS ***GONE!*** FOUR THOUSAND PEOPLE! NOT JUST SOLDIERS, DOCTORS, NURSES, TEACHERS!
BECAUSE OF YOU! BECAUSE OF ***YOUR*** HUBRIS!

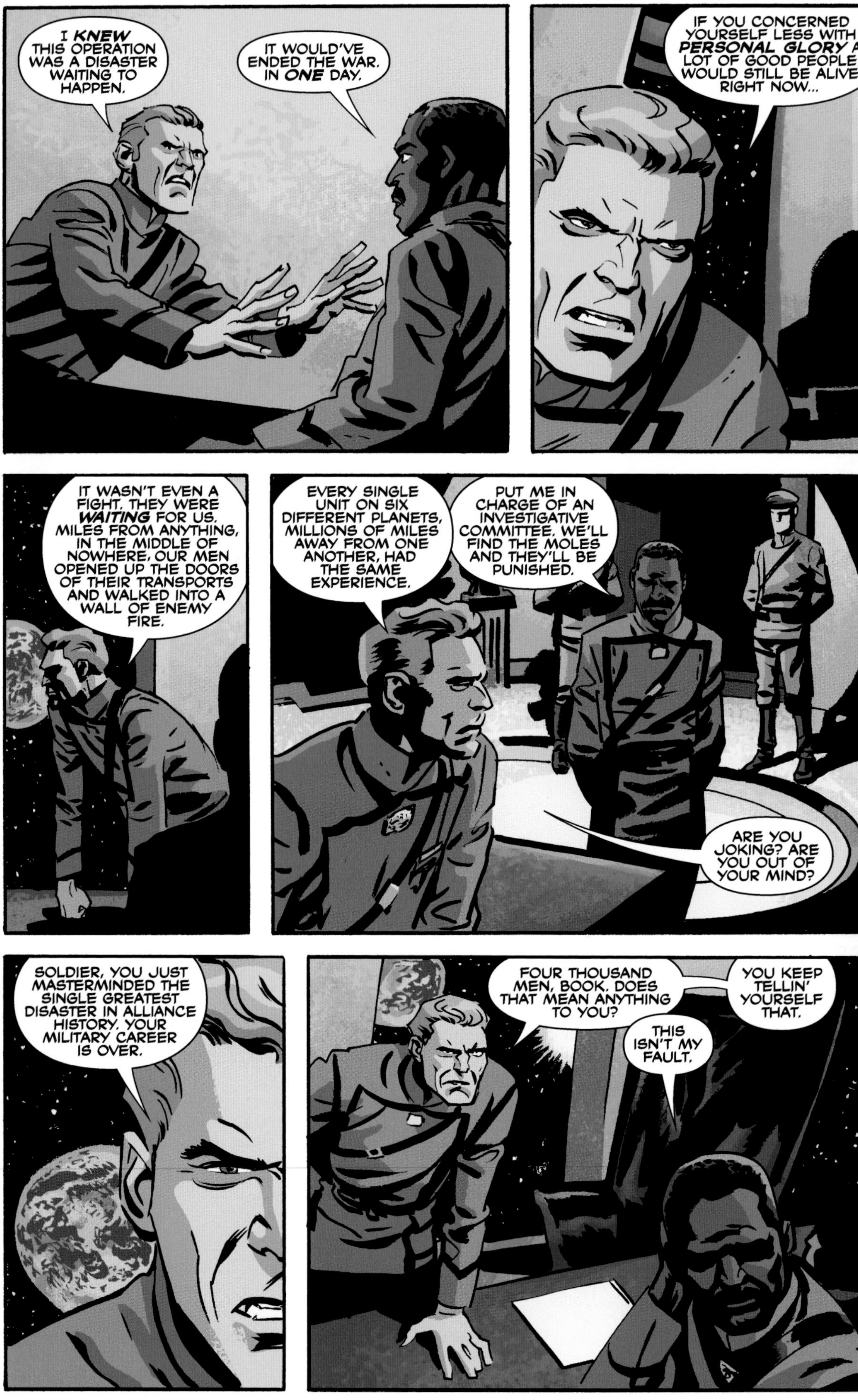
I *KNEW* THIS OPERATION WAS A DISASTER WAITING TO HAPPEN.
IT WOULD'VE ENDED THE WAR. IN *ONE* DAY.
IF YOU CONCERNED YOURSELF LESS WITH *PERSONAL GLORY* A LOT OF GOOD PEOPLE WOULD STILL BE ALIVE RIGHT NOW...
IT WASN'T EVEN A FIGHT. THEY WERE *WAITING* FOR US. MILES FROM ANYTHING, IN THE MIDDLE OF NOWHERE, OUR MEN OPENED UP THE DOORS OF THEIR TRANSPORTS AND WALKED INTO A WALL OF ENEMY FIRE.
EVERY SINGLE UNIT ON SIX DIFFERENT PLANETS, MILLIONS OF MILES AWAY FROM ONE ANOTHER, HAD THE SAME EXPERIENCE.
PUT ME IN CHARGE OF AN INVESTIGATIVE COMMITTEE. WE'LL FIND THE MOLES AND THEY'LL BE PUNISHED.
ARE YOU JOKING? ARE YOU OUT OF YOUR MIND?
SOLDIER, YOU JUST MASTERMINDED THE SINGLE GREATEST DISASTER IN ALLIANCE HISTORY. YOUR MILITARY CAREER IS OVER.
FOUR THOUSAND MEN, BOOK. DOES THAT MEAN ANYTHING TO YOU?
THIS ISN'T MY FAULT.
YOU KEEP TELLIN' YOURSELF THAT.

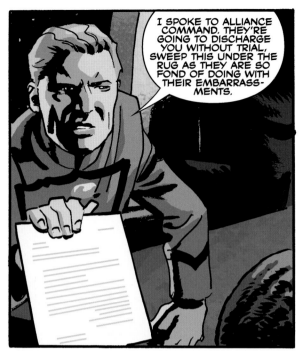

I SPOKE TO ALLIANCE COMMAND. THEY'RE GOING TO DISCHARGE YOU WITHOUT TRIAL, SWEEP THIS UNDER THE RUG AS THEY ARE SO FOND OF DOING WITH THEIR EMBARRASSMENTS.

WHICH IS EXACTLY WHAT YOU ARE. AN EMBARRASSMENT TO ANYONE WHO HAS EVER WORN THAT UNIFORM.

RRRIP

I WANT YOU OFF MY SHIP IMMEDIATELY.

I'LL TAKE THE NEXT SHUTTLE.

NO, I SAID IMMEDIATELY. THESE MEN WILL ESCORT YOU TO AN ESCAPE VESSEL.

WHAT? YOU'RE NOT SERIOUS. THOSE THINGS ARE DEATH-TRAPS.

A HAPPY COINCIDENCE.

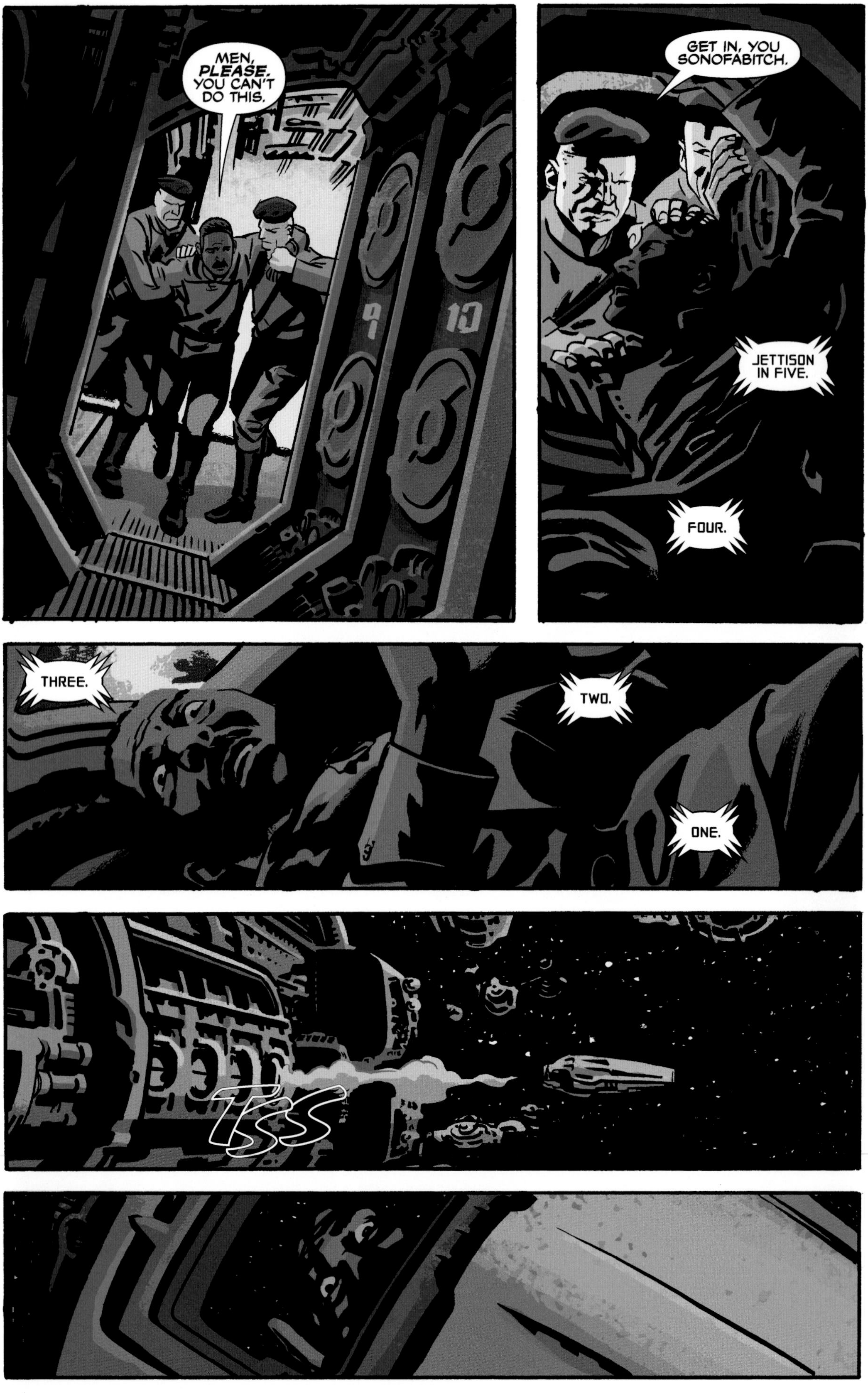
MEN, PLEASE. YOU CAN'T DO THIS.
9
10
GET IN, YOU SONOFABITCH.
JETTISON IN FIVE.
FOUR.
THREE.
TWO.
ONE.
TSS

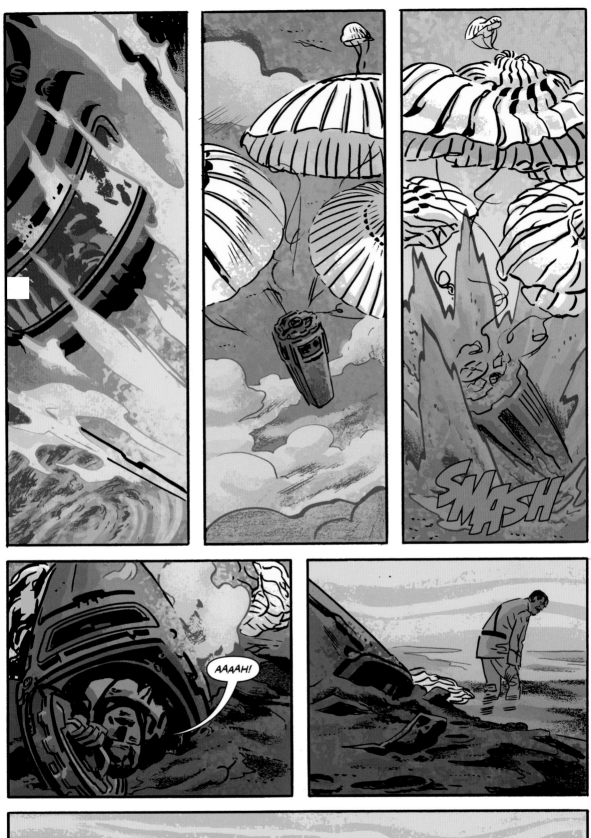

AAAAH!

"YOU'RE ALL ALONE. NO ONE'S GONNA SAVE YOU."

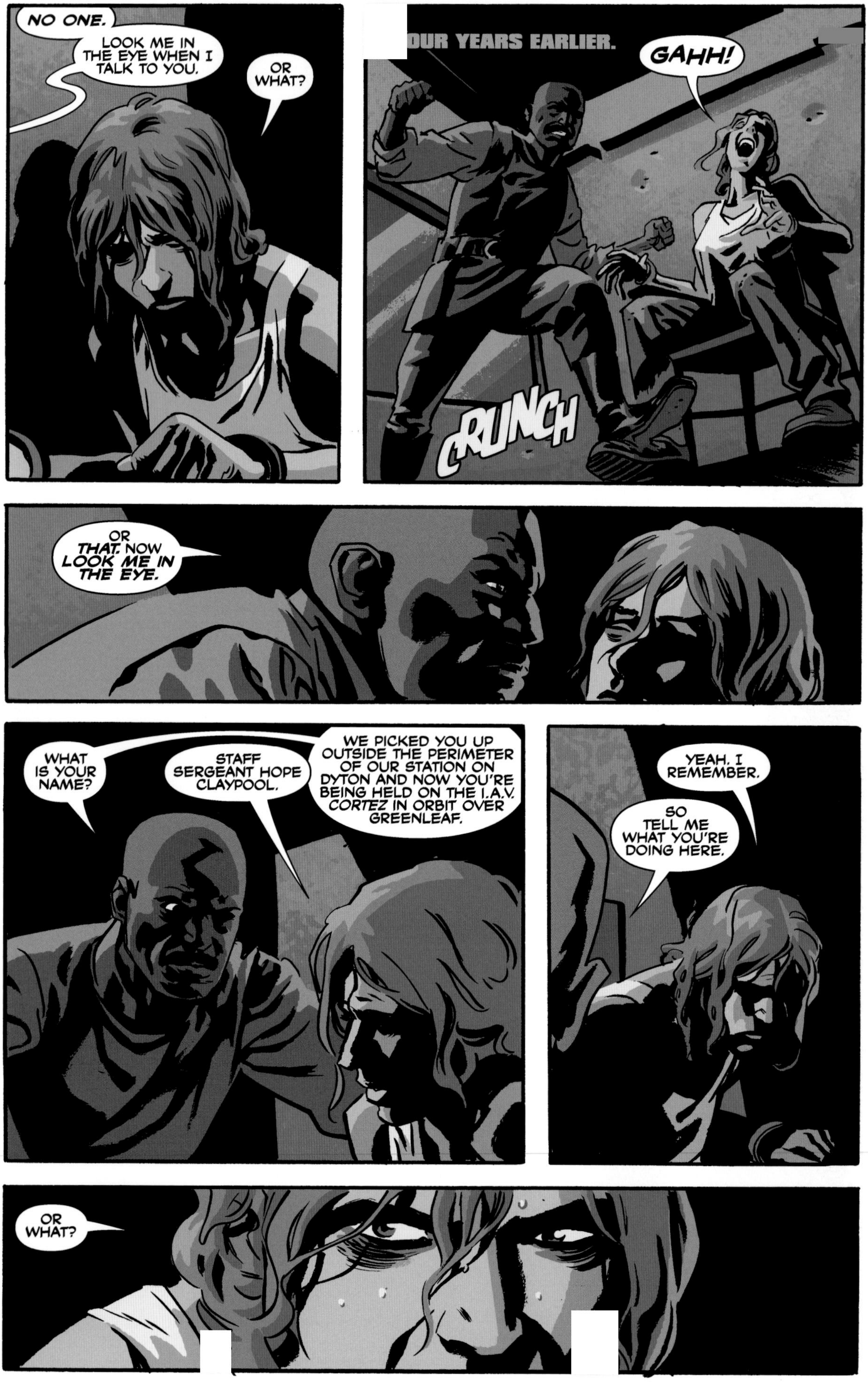
NO ONE.
LOOK ME IN THE EYE WHEN I TALK TO YOU.
OR WHAT?
OUR YEARS EARLIER.
GAHH!
CRUNCH
OR THAT. NOW LOOK ME IN THE EYE.
WHAT IS YOUR NAME?
STAFF SERGEANT HOPE CLAYPOOL.
WE PICKED YOU UP OUTSIDE THE PERIMETER OF OUR STATION ON DYTON AND NOW YOU'RE BEING HELD ON THE I.A.V. CORTEZ IN ORBIT OVER GREENLEAF.
YEAH. I REMEMBER.
SO TELL ME WHAT YOU'RE DOING HERE.
OR WHAT?

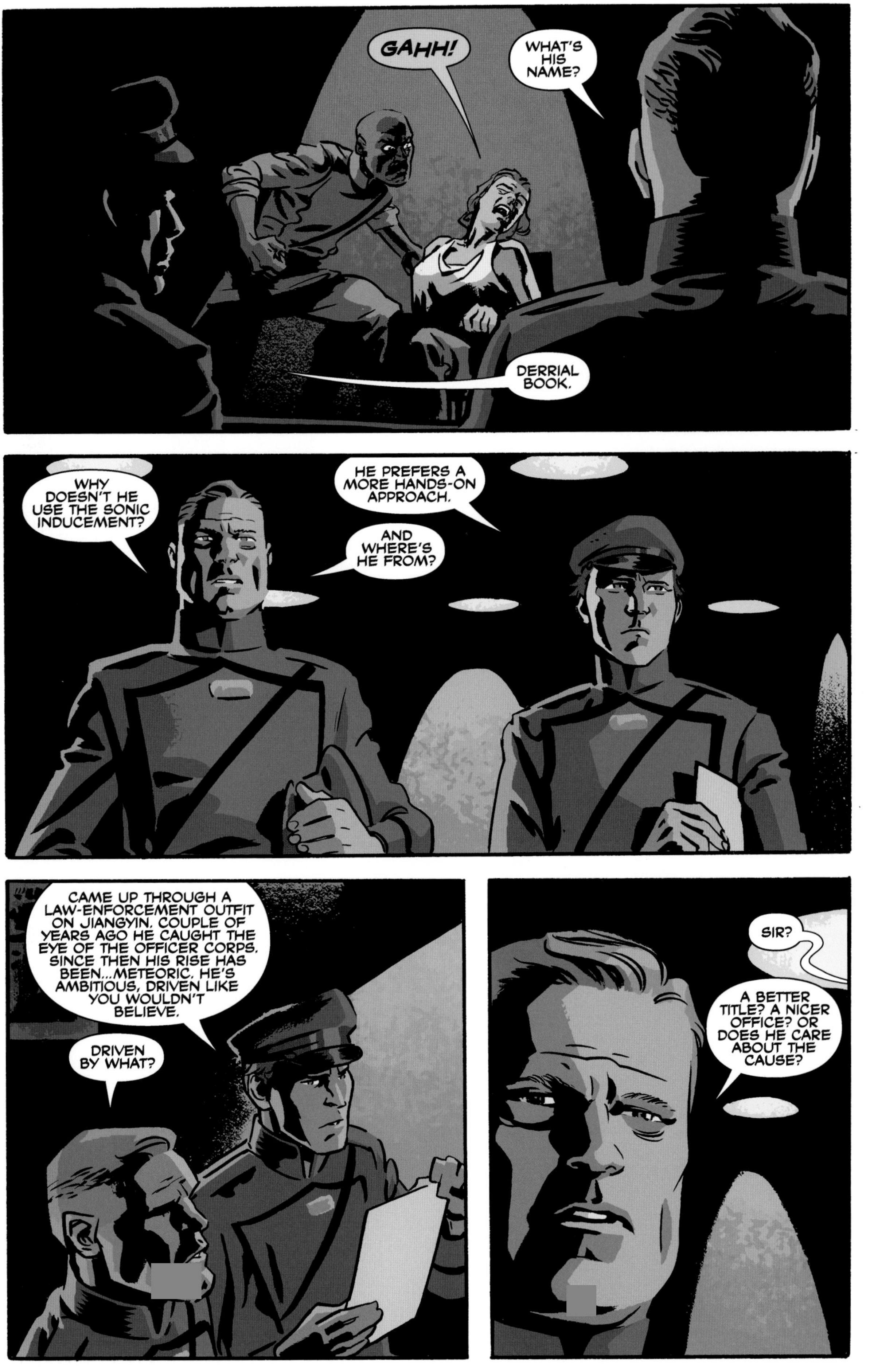
GAHH!
WHAT'S HIS NAME?
DERRIAL BOOK.
WHY DOESN'T HE USE THE SONIC INDUCEMENT?
HE PREFERS A MORE HANDS-ON APPROACH.
AND WHERE'S HE FROM?
CAME UP THROUGH A LAW-ENFORCEMENT OUTFIT ON JIANGYIN. COUPLE OF YEARS AGO HE CAUGHT THE EYE OF THE OFFICER CORPS. SINCE THEN HIS RISE HAS BEEN...METEORIC. HE'S AMBITIOUS, DRIVEN LIKE YOU WOULDN'T BELIEVE.
DRIVEN BY WHAT?
SIR?
A BETTER TITLE? A NICER OFFICE? OR DOES HE CARE ABOUT THE CAUSE?

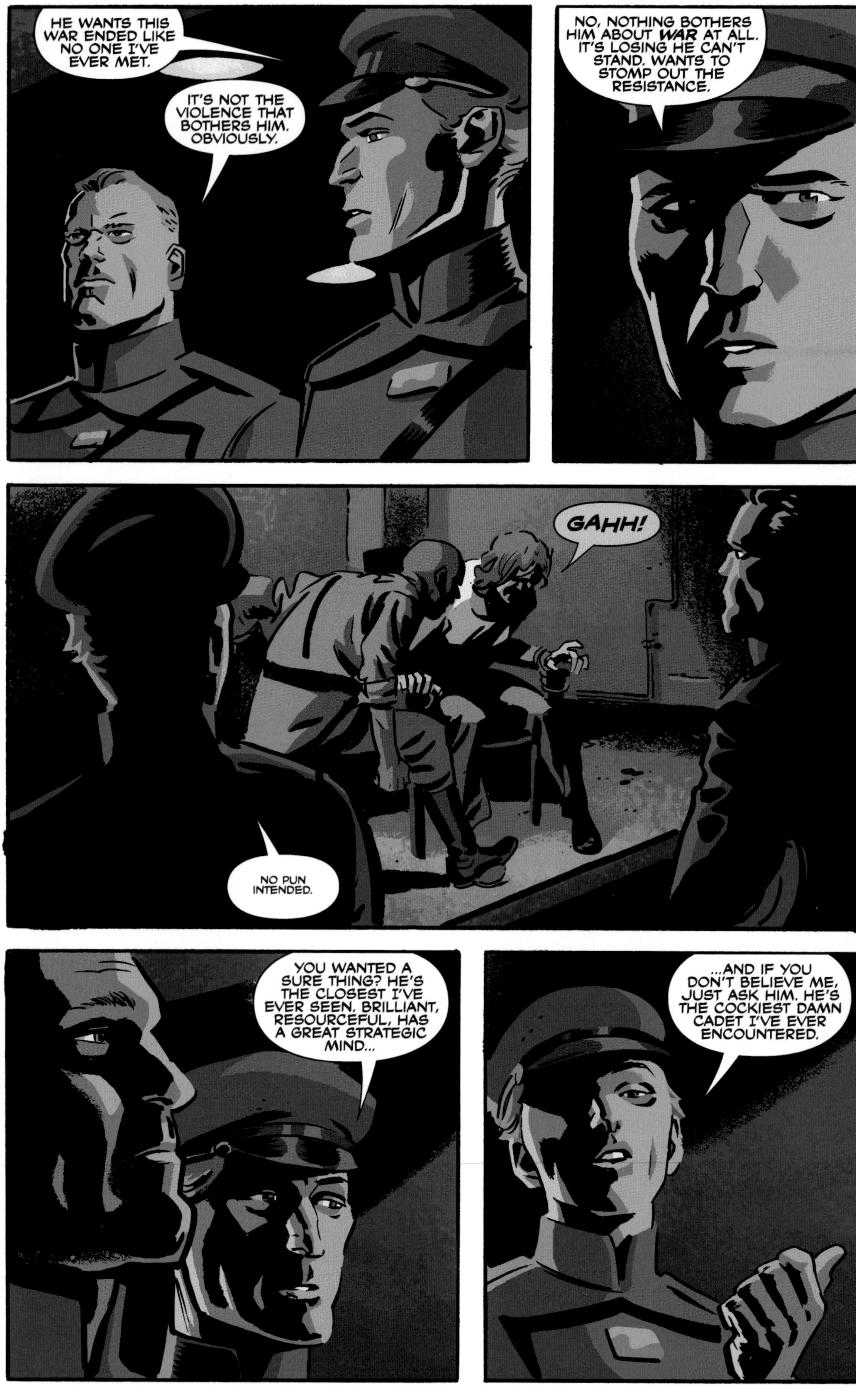
HE WANTS THIS WAR ENDED LIKE NO ONE I'VE EVER MET.
IT'S NOT THE VIOLENCE THAT BOTHERS HIM. OBVIOUSLY.
NO, NOTHING BOTHERS HIM ABOUT ***WAR*** AT ALL. IT'S LOSING HE CAN'T STAND. WANTS TO STOMP OUT THE RESISTANCE.
GAHH!
NO PUN INTENDED.
YOU WANTED A SURE THING? HE'S THE CLOSEST I'VE EVER SEEN. BRILLIANT, RESOURCEFUL, HAS A GREAT STRATEGIC MIND...
...AND IF YOU DON'T BELIEVE ME, JUST ASK HIM. HE'S THE COCKIEST DAMN CADET I'VE EVER ENCOUNTERED.

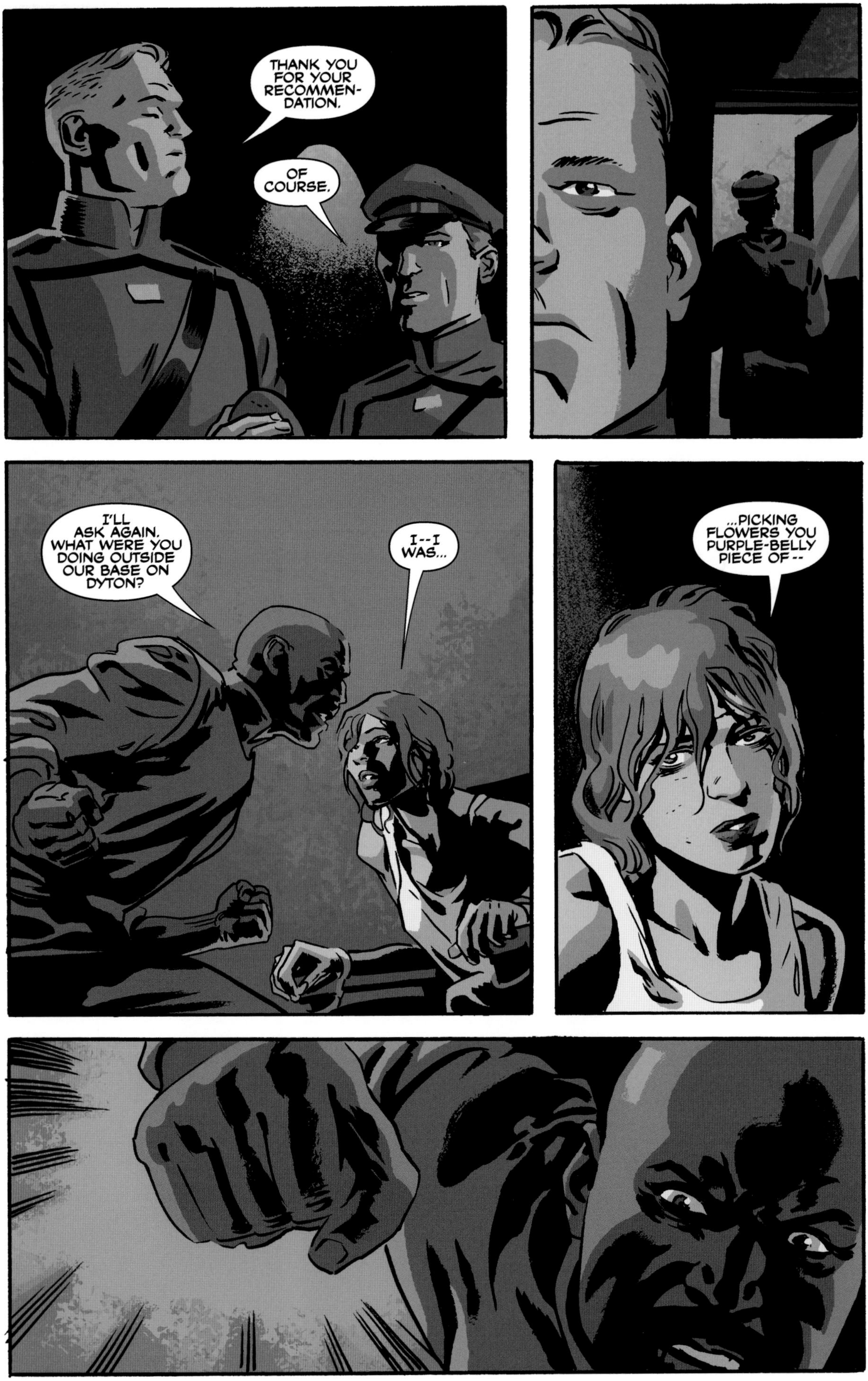
THANK YOU FOR YOUR RECOMMEN-DATION.
OF COURSE.
I'LL ASK AGAIN. WHAT WERE YOU DOING OUTSIDE OUR BASE ON DYTON?
I--I WAS...
...PICKING FLOWERS YOU PURPLE-BELLY PIECE OF --

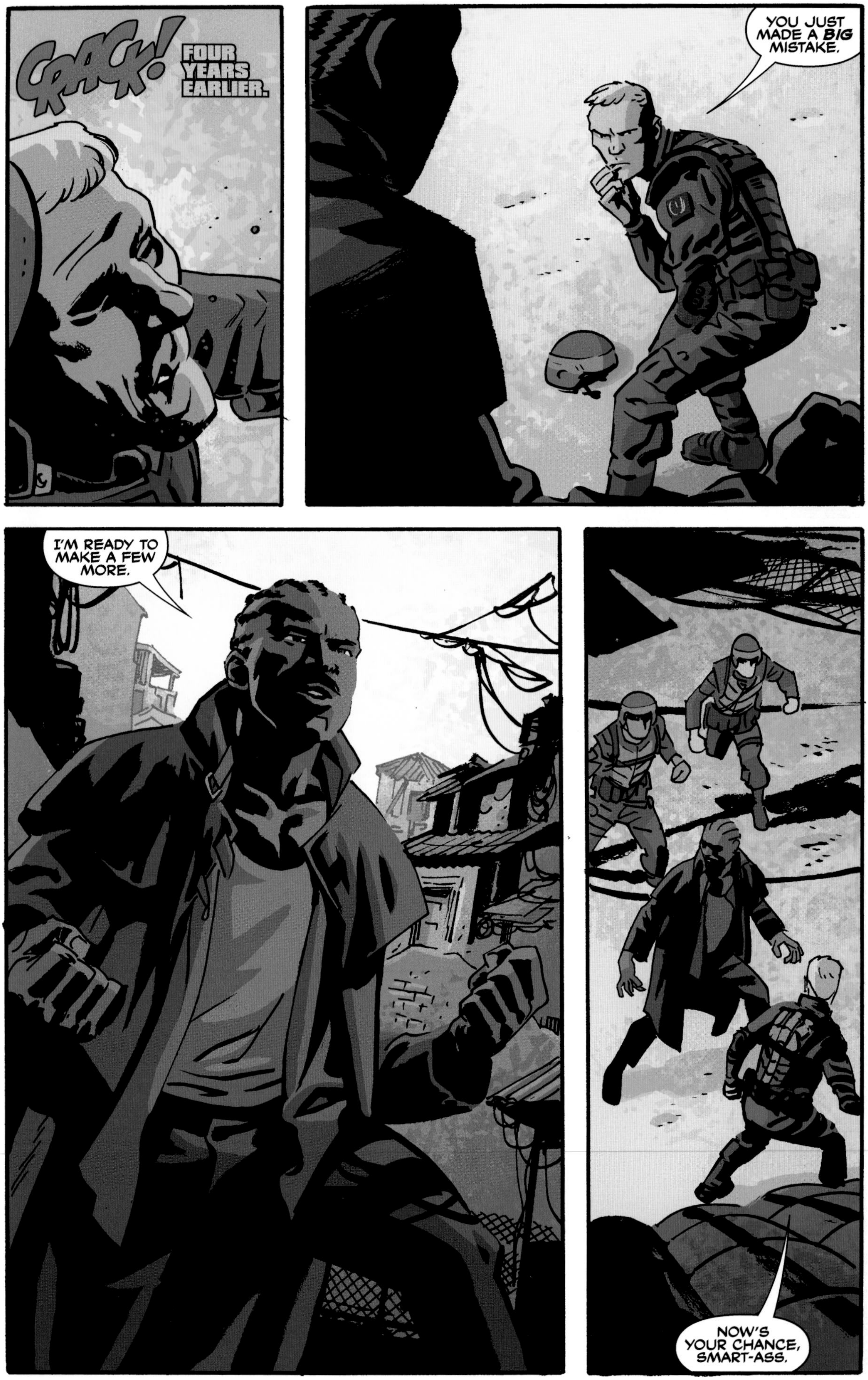
CRACK!
FOUR YEARS EARLIER.
YOU JUST MADE A BIG MISTAKE.
I'M READY TO MAKE A FEW MORE.
NOW'S YOUR CHANCE, SMART-ASS.

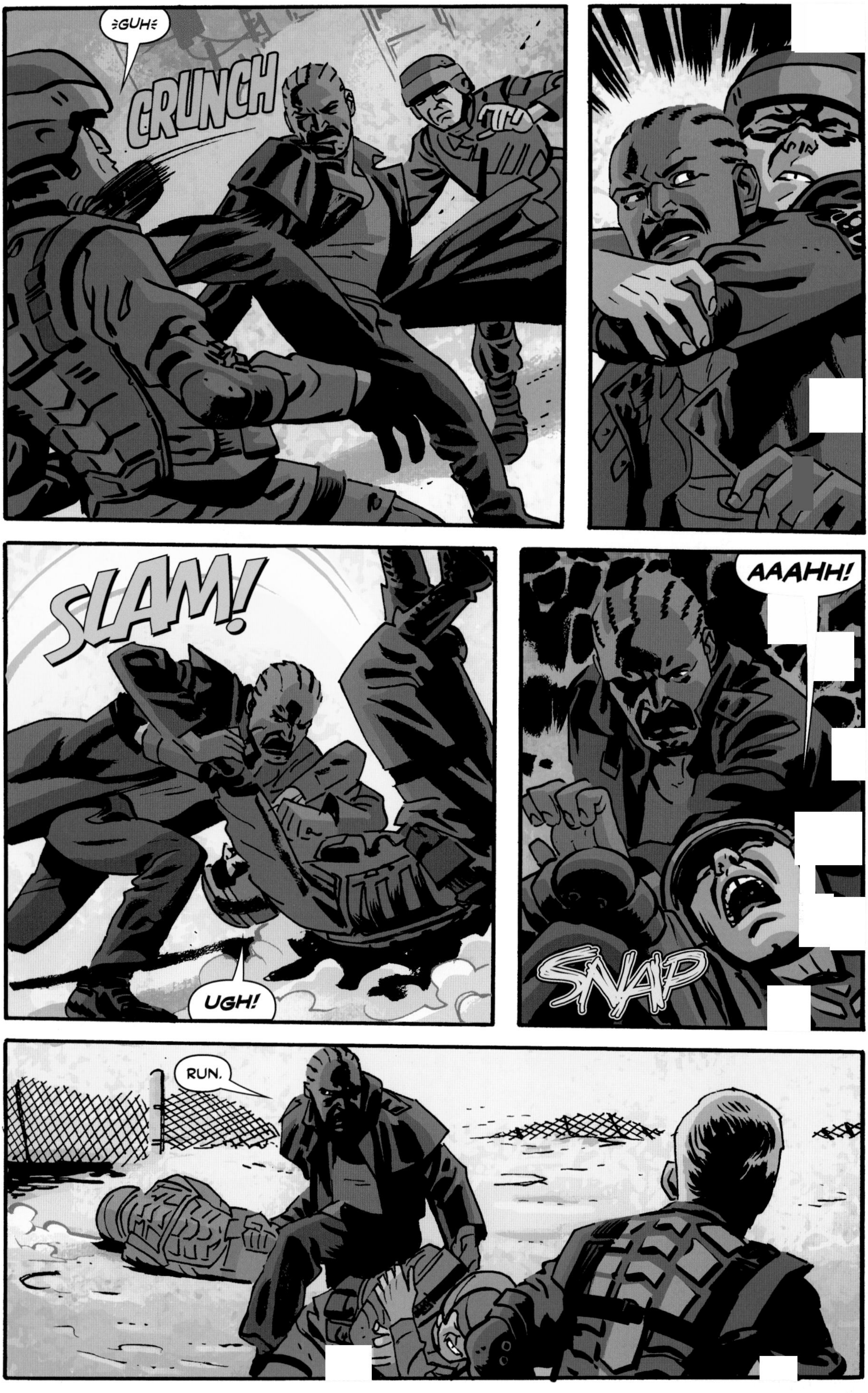
GUH
CRUNCH
SLAM!
UGH!
AAAHH!
SNAP
RUN.

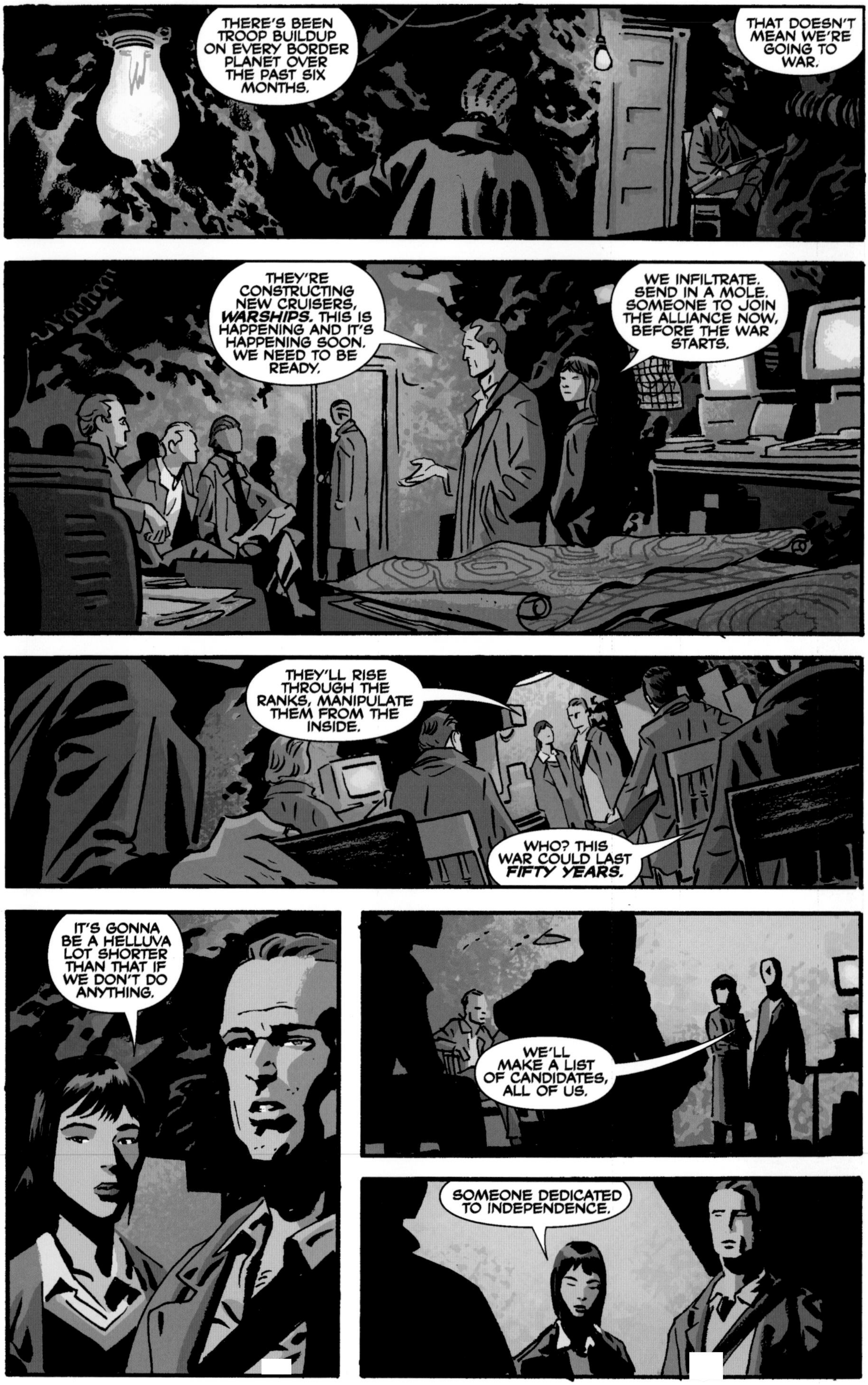
THERE'S BEEN TROOP BUILDUP ON EVERY BORDER PLANET OVER THE PAST SIX MONTHS.
THAT DOESN'T MEAN WE'RE GOING TO WAR.
THEY'RE CONSTRUCTING NEW CRUISERS, WARSHIPS. THIS IS HAPPENING AND IT'S HAPPENING SOON. WE NEED TO BE READY.
WE INFILTRATE. SEND IN A MOLE. SOMEONE TO JOIN THE ALLIANCE NOW, BEFORE THE WAR STARTS.
THEY'LL RISE THROUGH THE RANKS, MANIPULATE THEM FROM THE INSIDE.
WHO? THIS WAR COULD LAST FIFTY YEARS.
IT'S GONNA BE A HELLUVA LOT SHORTER THAN THAT IF WE DON'T DO ANYTHING.
WE'LL MAKE A LIST OF CANDIDATES, ALL OF US.
SOMEONE DEDICATED TO INDEPENDENCE.

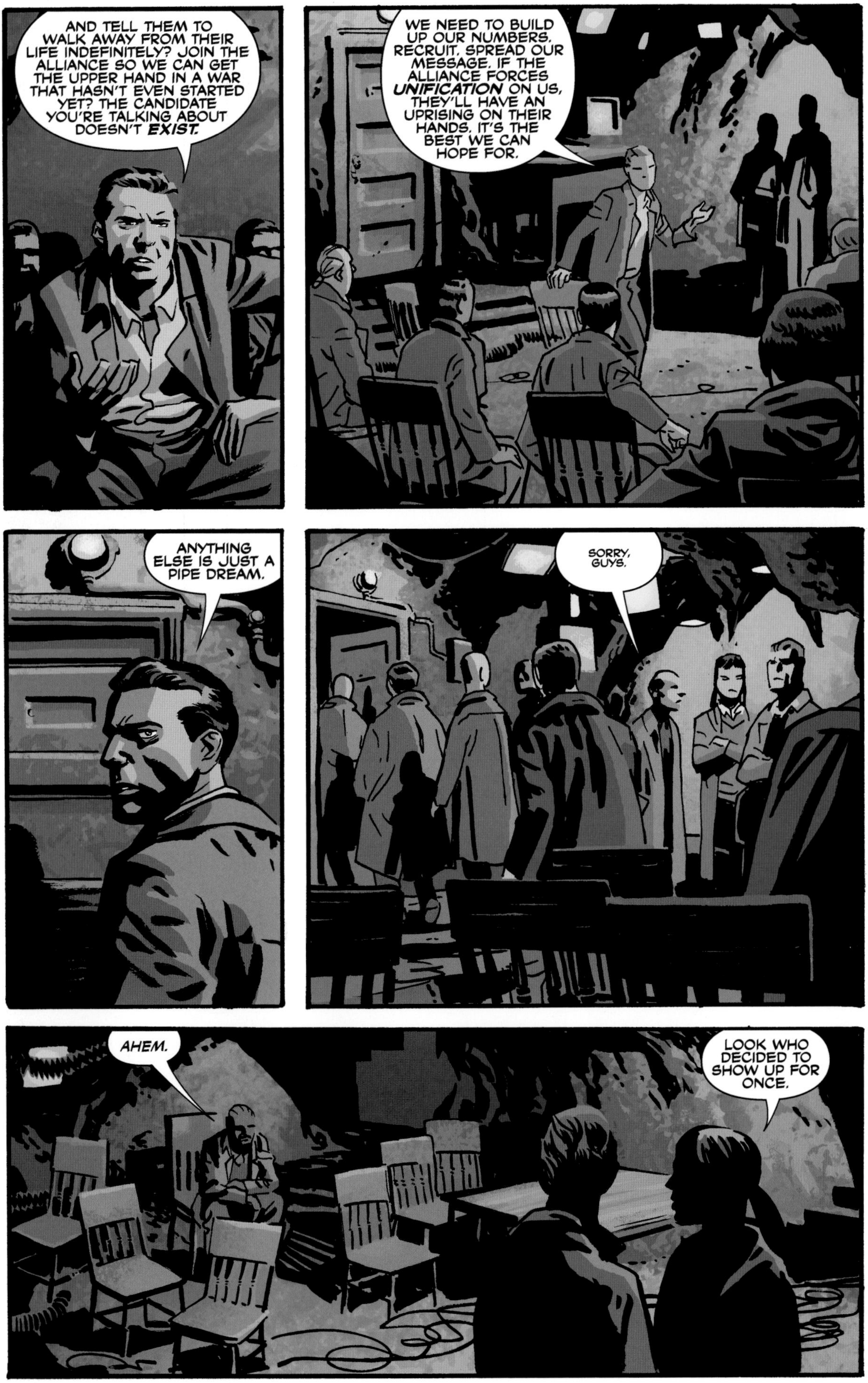
AND TELL THEM TO WALK AWAY FROM THEIR LIFE INDEFINITELY? JOIN THE ALLIANCE SO WE CAN GET THE UPPER HAND IN A WAR THAT HASN'T EVEN STARTED YET? THE CANDIDATE YOU'RE TALKING ABOUT DOESN'T *EXIST.*
WE NEED TO BUILD UP OUR NUMBERS. RECRUIT. SPREAD OUR MESSAGE. IF THE ALLIANCE FORCES *UNIFICATION* ON US, THEY'LL HAVE AN UPRISING ON THEIR HANDS. IT'S THE BEST WE CAN HOPE FOR.
ANYTHING ELSE IS JUST A PIPE DREAM.
SORRY, GUYS.
AHEM.
LOOK WHO DECIDED TO SHOW UP FOR ONCE.

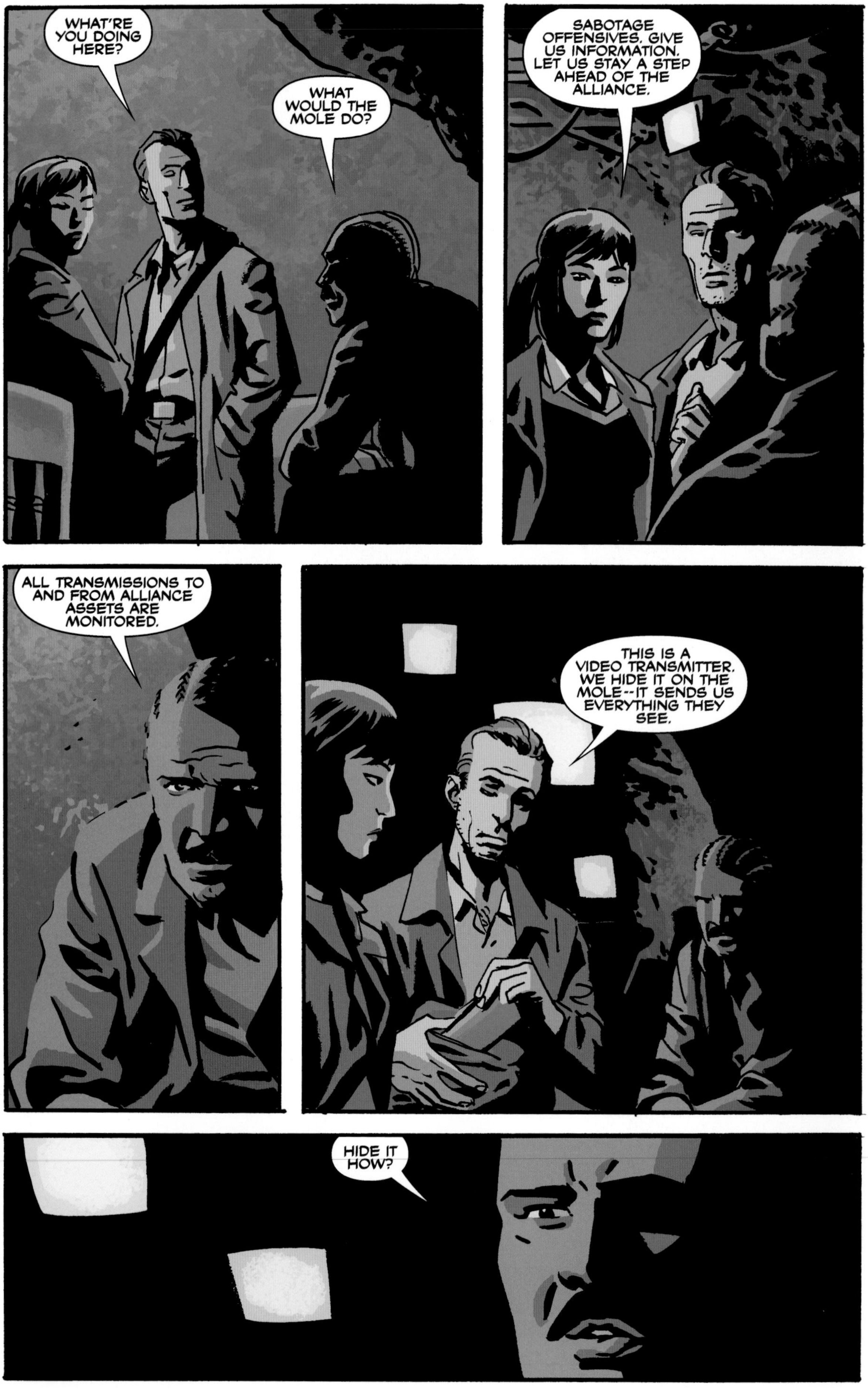
WHAT'RE YOU DOING HERE?
WHAT WOULD THE MOLE DO?
SABOTAGE OFFENSIVES. GIVE US INFORMATION. LET US STAY A STEP AHEAD OF THE ALLIANCE.
ALL TRANSMISSIONS TO AND FROM ALLIANCE ASSETS ARE MONITORED.
THIS IS A VIDEO TRANSMITTER. WE HIDE IT ON THE MOLE--IT SENDS US EVERYTHING THEY SEE.
HIDE IT HOW?

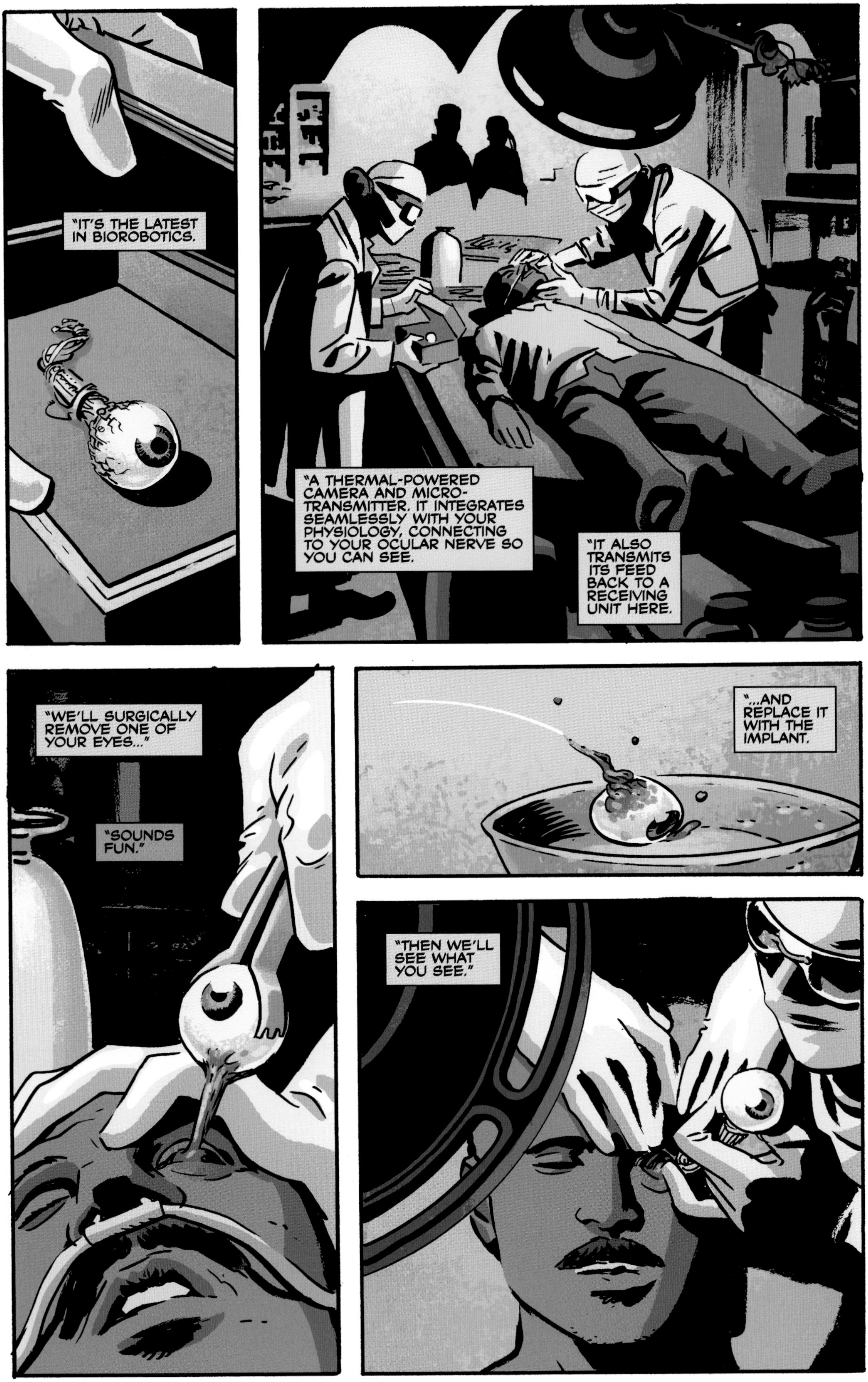
"IT'S THE LATEST IN BIOROBOTICS.
"A THERMAL-POWERED CAMERA AND MICRO-TRANSMITTER. IT INTEGRATES SEAMLESSLY WITH YOUR PHYSIOLOGY, CONNECTING TO YOUR OCULAR NERVE SO YOU CAN SEE.
"IT ALSO TRANSMITS ITS FEED BACK TO A RECEIVING UNIT HERE.
"WE'LL SURGICALLY REMOVE ONE OF YOUR EYES..."
"SOUNDS FUN."
"...AND REPLACE IT WITH THE IMPLANT.
"THEN WE'LL SEE WHAT YOU SEE."

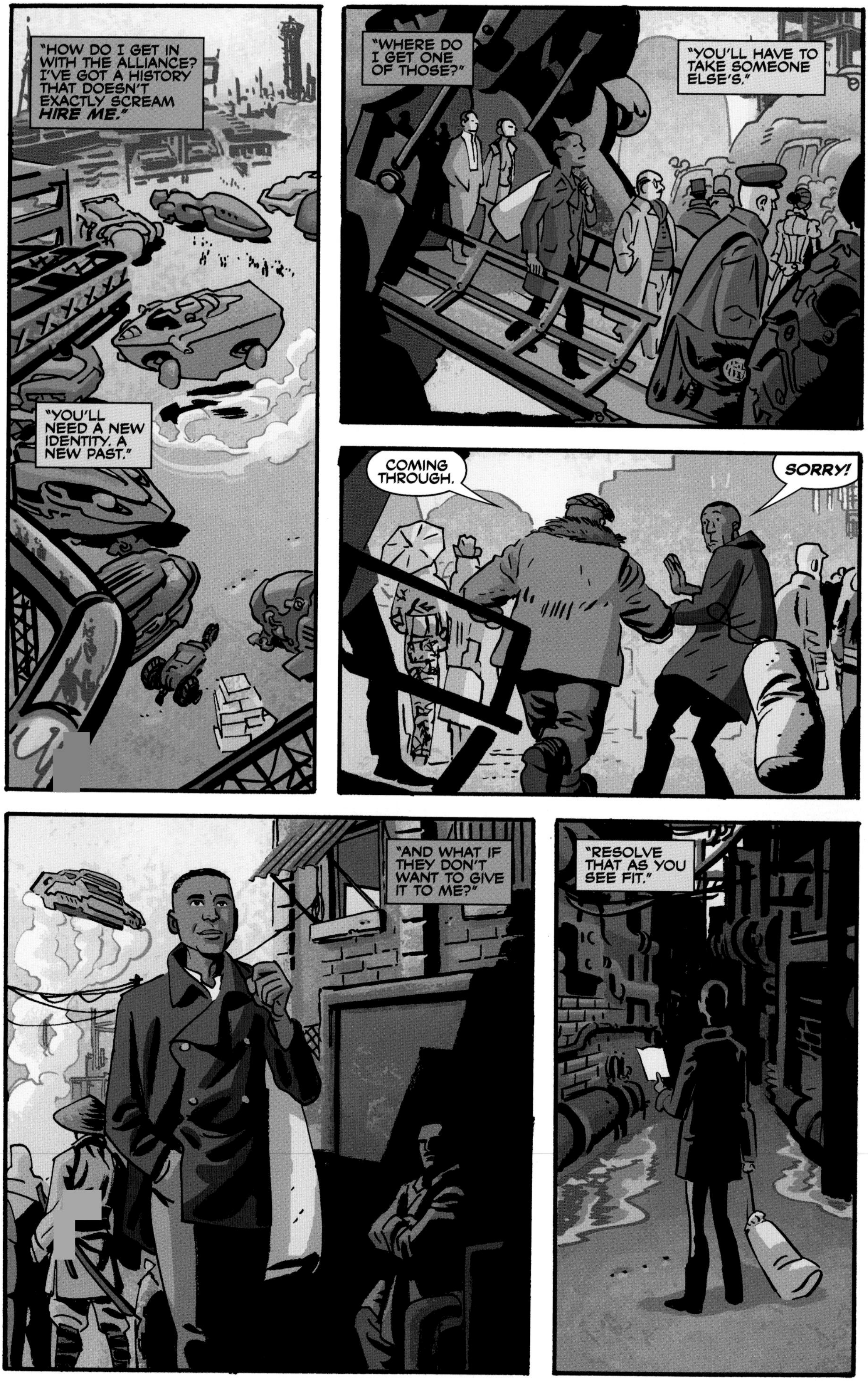
"HOW DO I GET IN WITH THE ALLIANCE? I'VE GOT A HISTORY THAT DOESN'T EXACTLY SCREAM *HIRE ME.*"
"YOU'LL NEED A NEW IDENTITY. A NEW PAST."
"WHERE DO I GET ONE OF THOSE?"
"YOU'LL HAVE TO TAKE SOMEONE ELSE'S."
COMING THROUGH.
SORRY!
"AND WHAT IF THEY DON'T WANT TO GIVE IT TO ME?"
"RESOLVE THAT AS YOU SEE FIT."

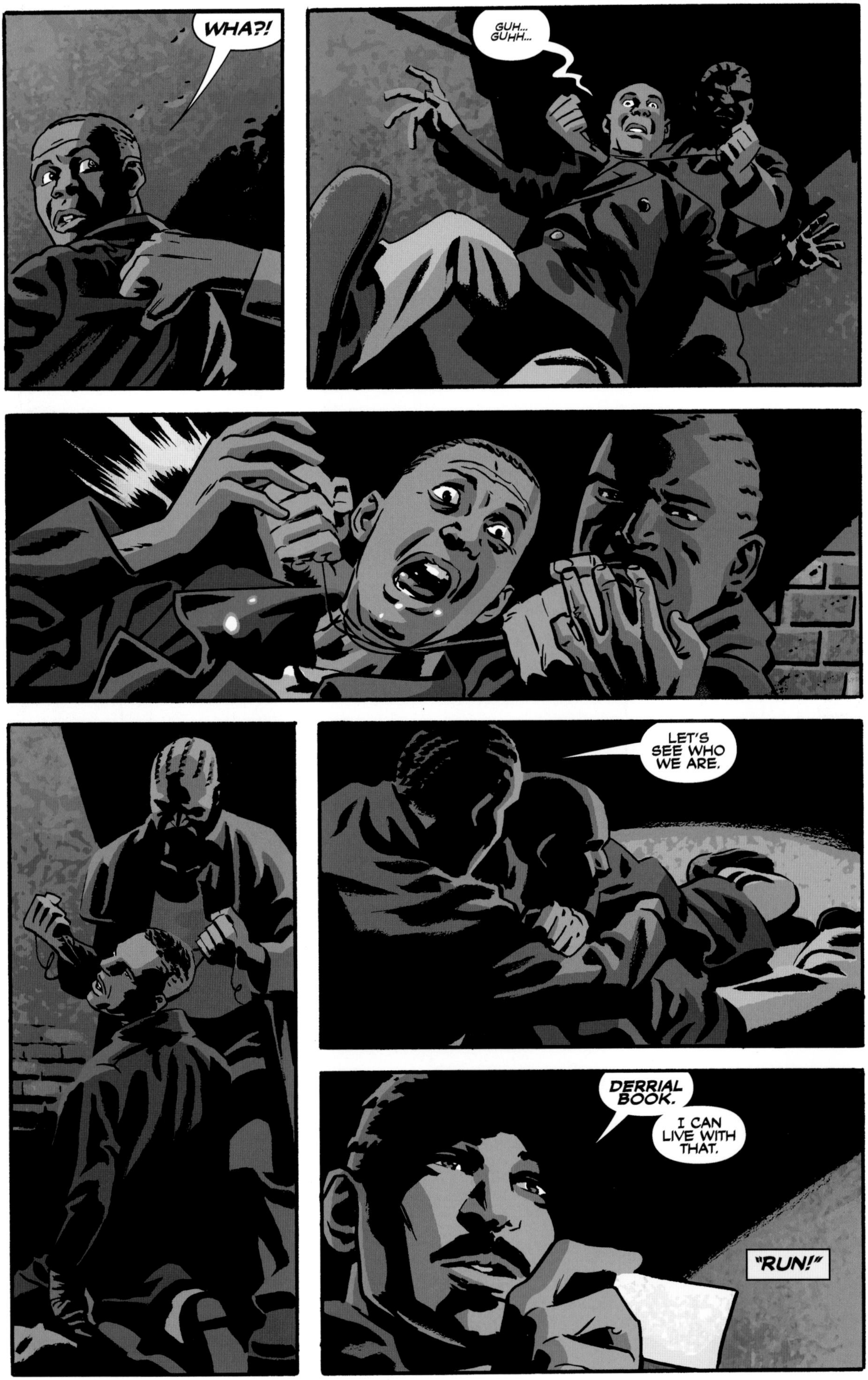
WHA?!
GUH... GUHH...
LET'S SEE WHO WE ARE.
DERRIAL BOOK.
I CAN LIVE WITH THAT.
"RUN!"

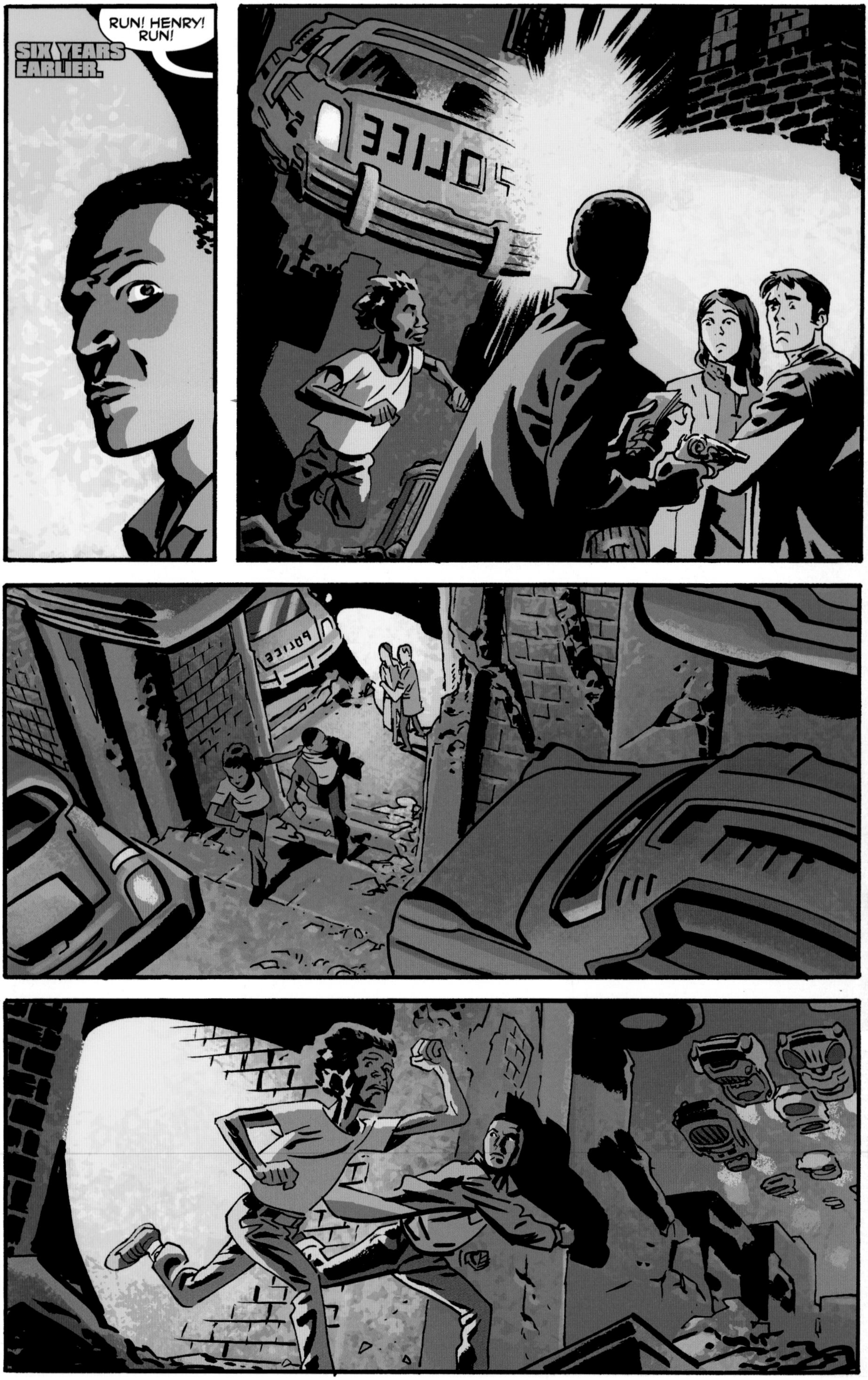
SIX YEARS EARLIER.
RUN! HENRY! RUN!
POLICE
POLICE

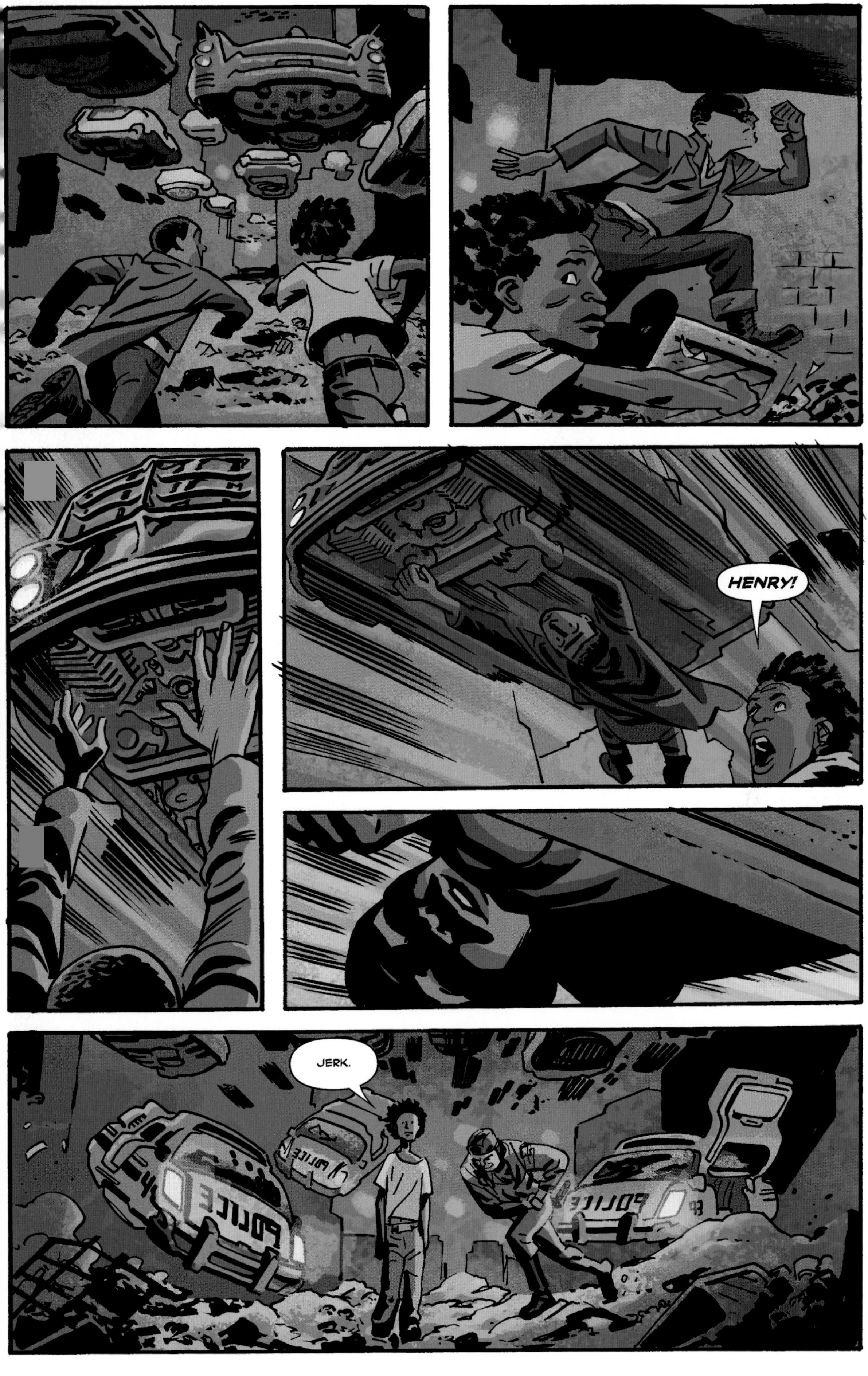
HENRY!
JERK.
POLICE
POLICE
POLICE

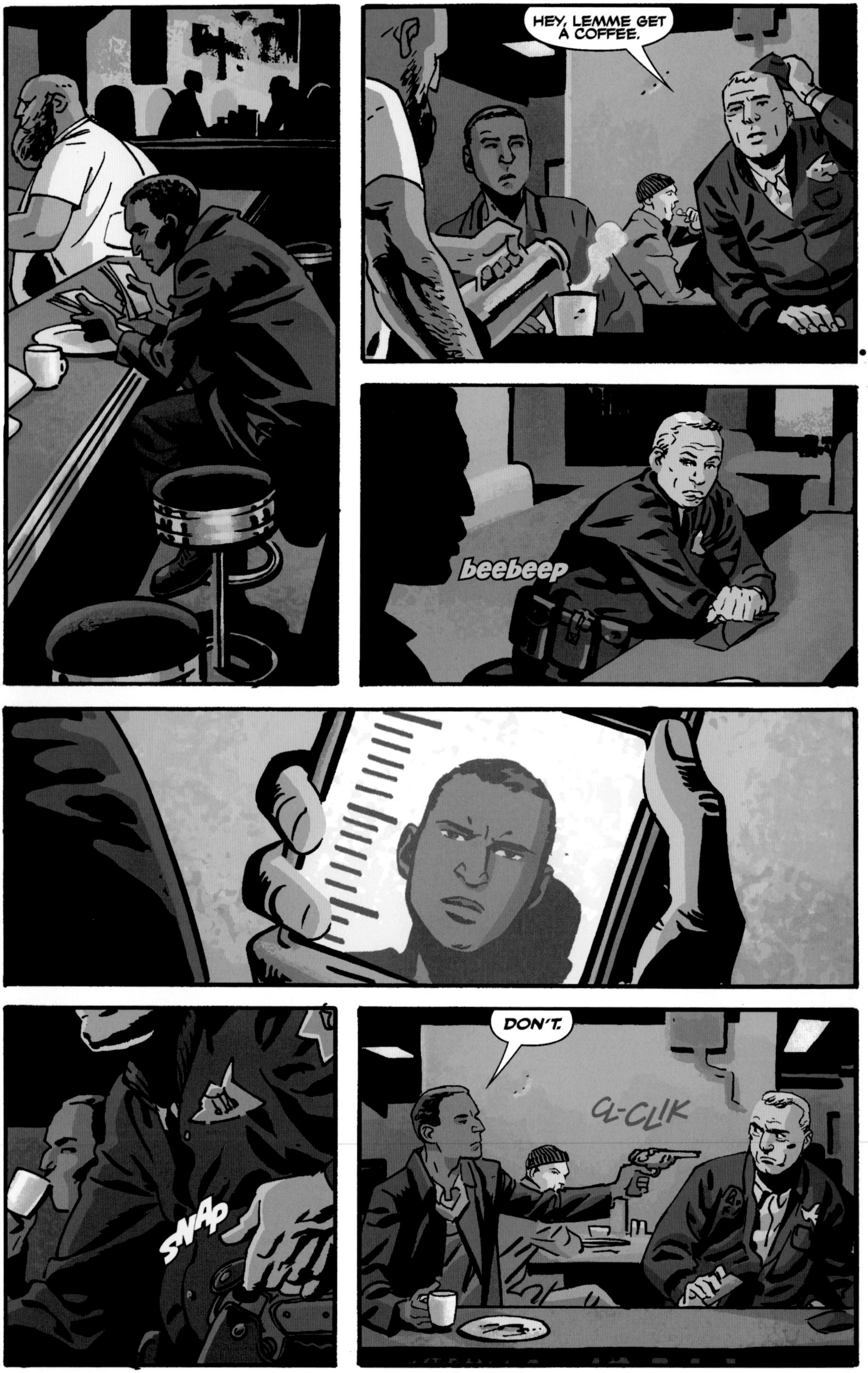
HEY, LEMME GET A COFFEE.
beebeep
SNAP
DON'T.
CL-CLIK

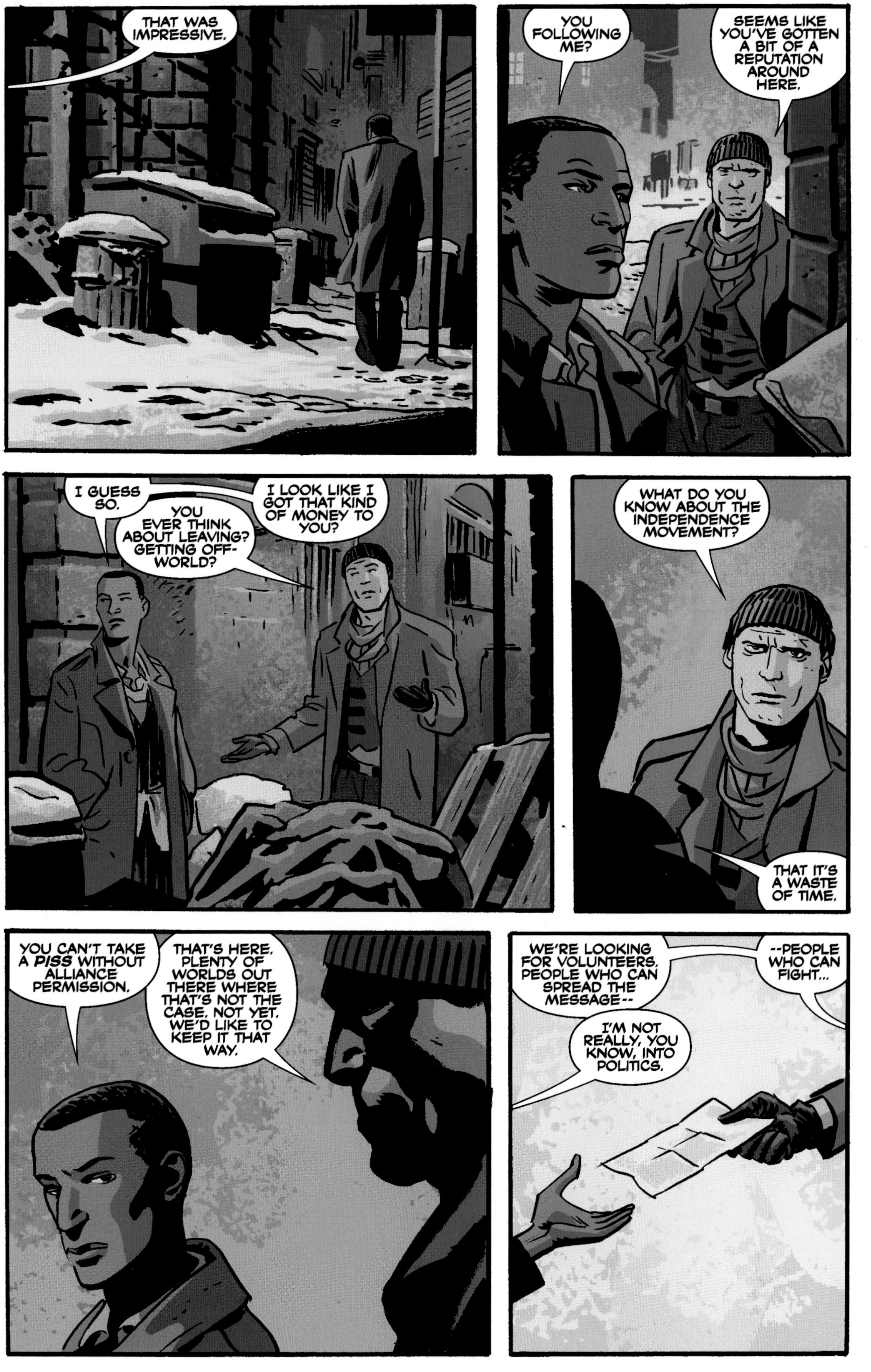
THAT WAS IMPRESSIVE.
YOU FOLLOWING ME?
SEEMS LIKE YOU'VE GOTTEN A BIT OF A REPUTATION AROUND HERE.
I GUESS SO.
YOU EVER THINK ABOUT LEAVING? GETTING OFF-WORLD?
I LOOK LIKE I GOT THAT KIND OF MONEY TO YOU?
WHAT DO YOU KNOW ABOUT THE INDEPENDENCE MOVEMENT?
THAT IT'S A WASTE OF TIME.
YOU CAN'T TAKE A PISS WITHOUT ALLIANCE PERMISSION.
THAT'S HERE. PLENTY OF WORLDS OUT THERE WHERE THAT'S NOT THE CASE. NOT YET. WE'D LIKE TO KEEP IT THAT WAY.
WE'RE LOOKING FOR VOLUNTEERS. PEOPLE WHO CAN SPREAD THE MESSAGE--
--PEOPLE WHO CAN FIGHT...
I'M NOT REALLY, YOU KNOW, INTO POLITICS.

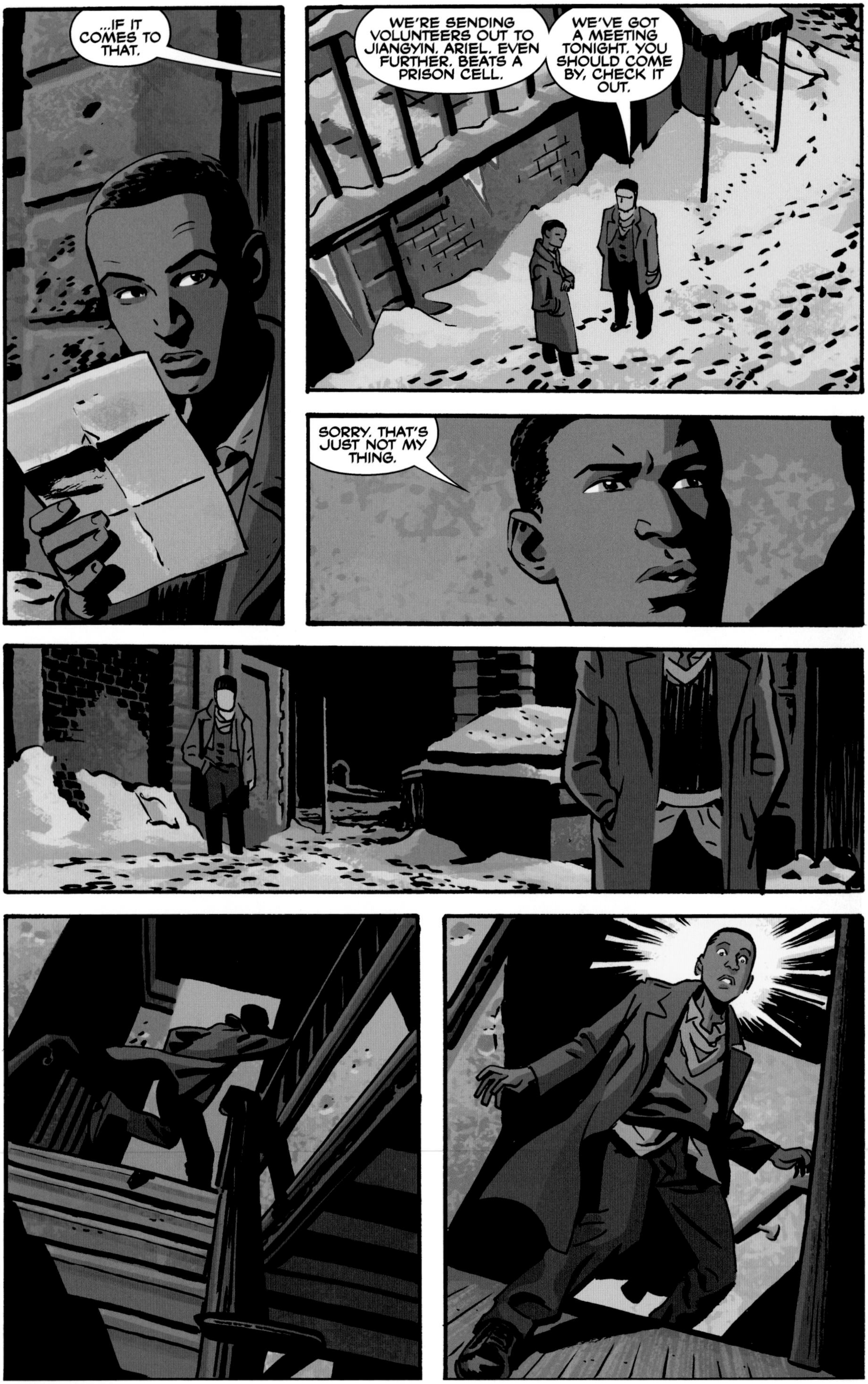
...IF IT COMES TO THAT.
WE'RE SENDING VOLUNTEERS OUT TO JIANGYIN, ARIEL. EVEN FURTHER. BEATS A PRISON CELL.
WE'VE GOT A MEETING TONIGHT. YOU SHOULD COME BY, CHECK IT OUT.
SORRY. THAT'S JUST NOT MY THING.

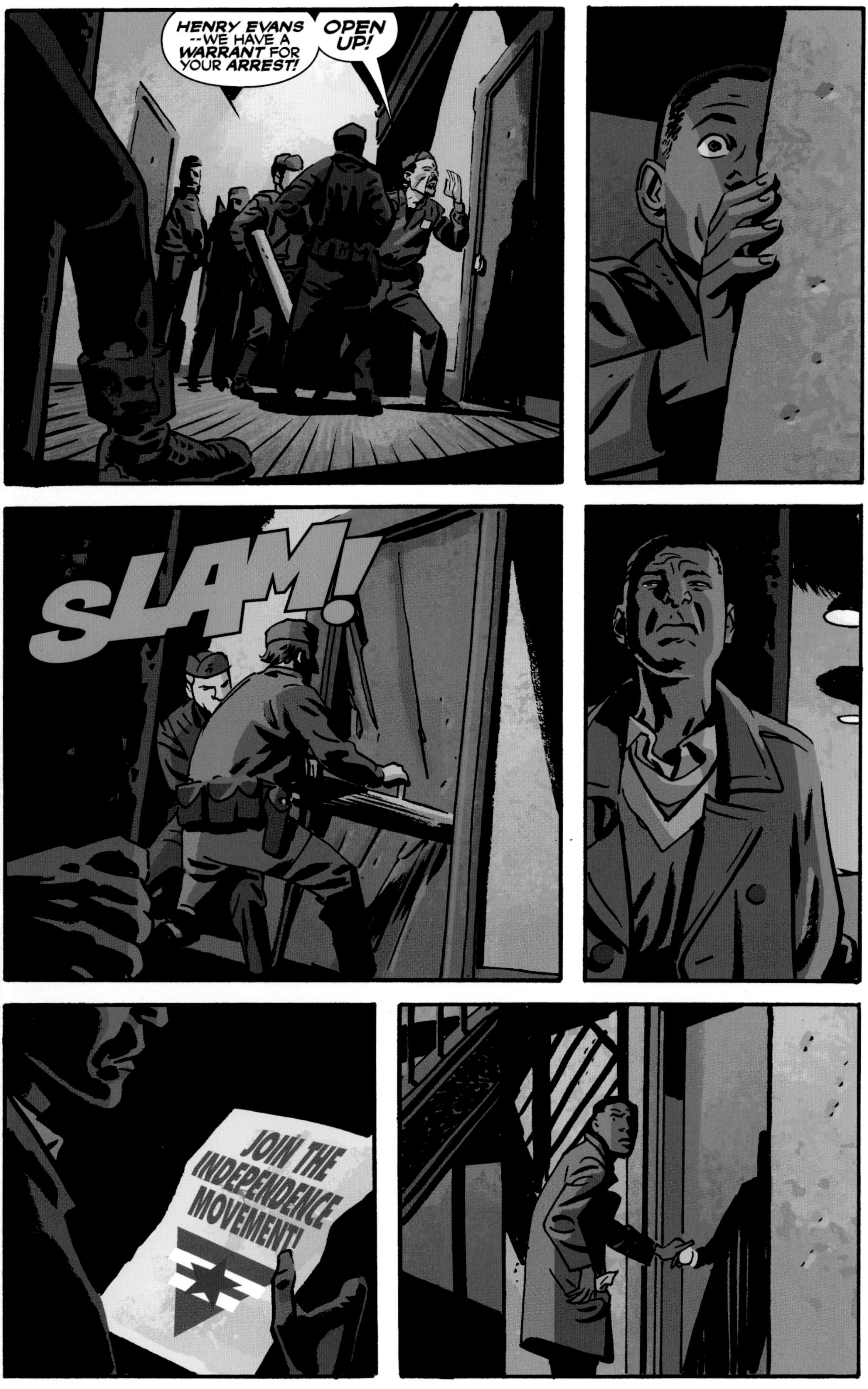
HENRY EVANS --WE HAVE A WARRANT FOR YOUR ARREST!
OPEN UP!
SLAM!
JOIN THE INDEPENDENCE MOVEMENT!

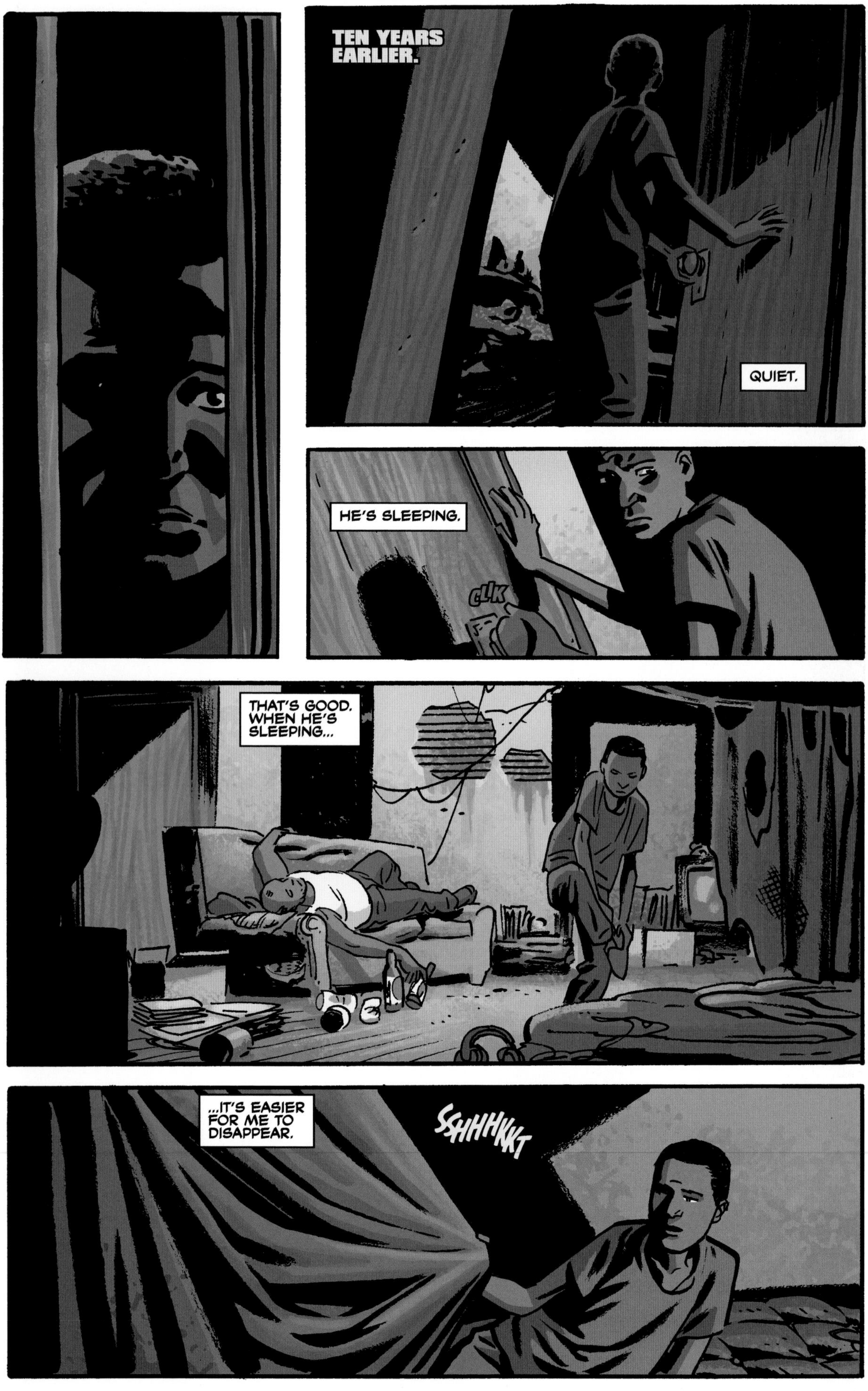
TEN YEARS EARLIER.
QUIET.
HE'S SLEEPING.
CLIK
THAT'S GOOD. WHEN HE'S SLEEPING...
...IT'S EASIER FOR ME TO DISAPPEAR.
SSHHHKKKT

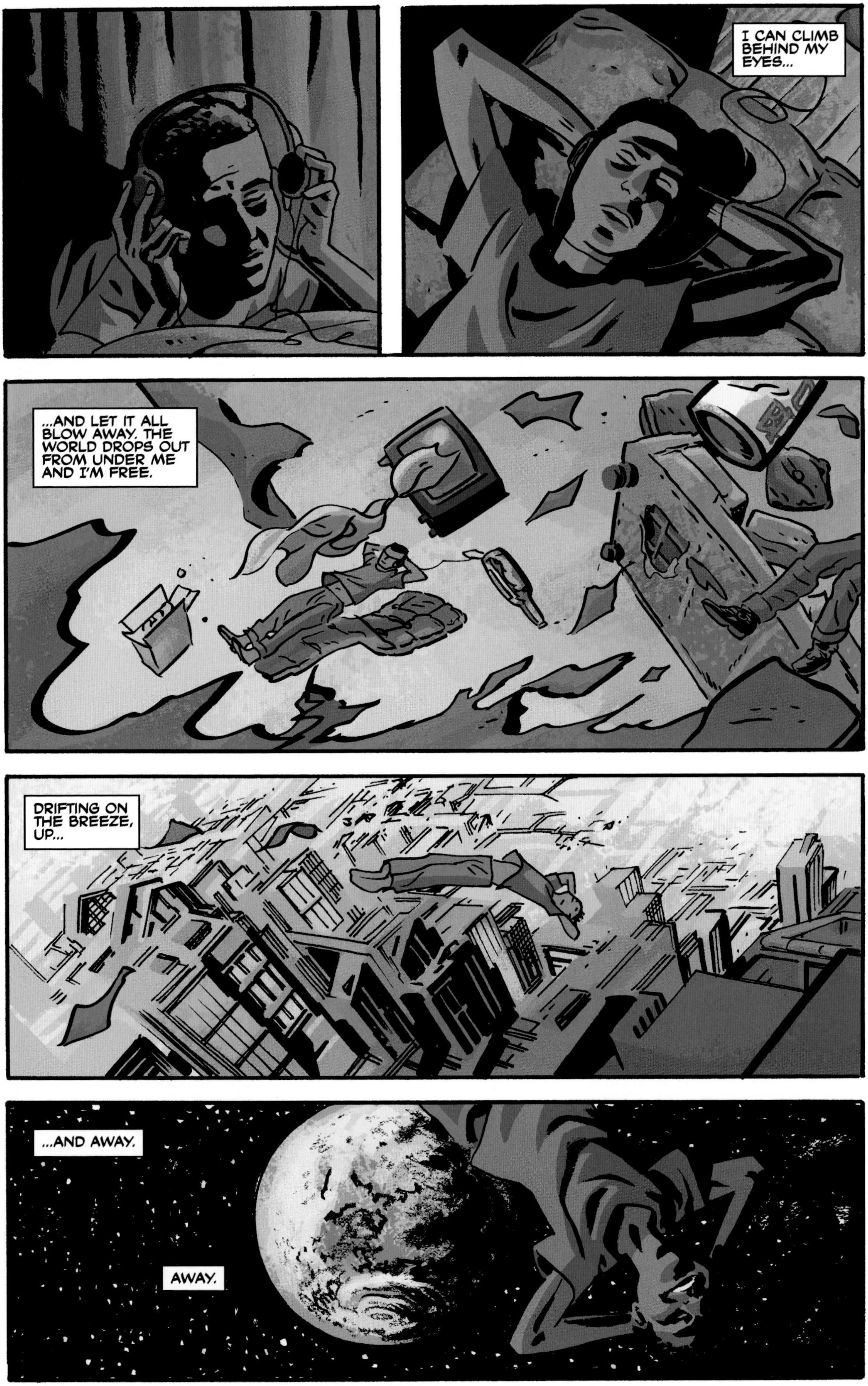
I CAN CLIMB BEHIND MY EYES...
...AND LET IT ALL BLOW AWAY. THE WORLD DROPS OUT FROM UNDER ME AND I'M FREE.
DRIFTING ON THE BREEZE, UP...
...AND AWAY.
AWAY.

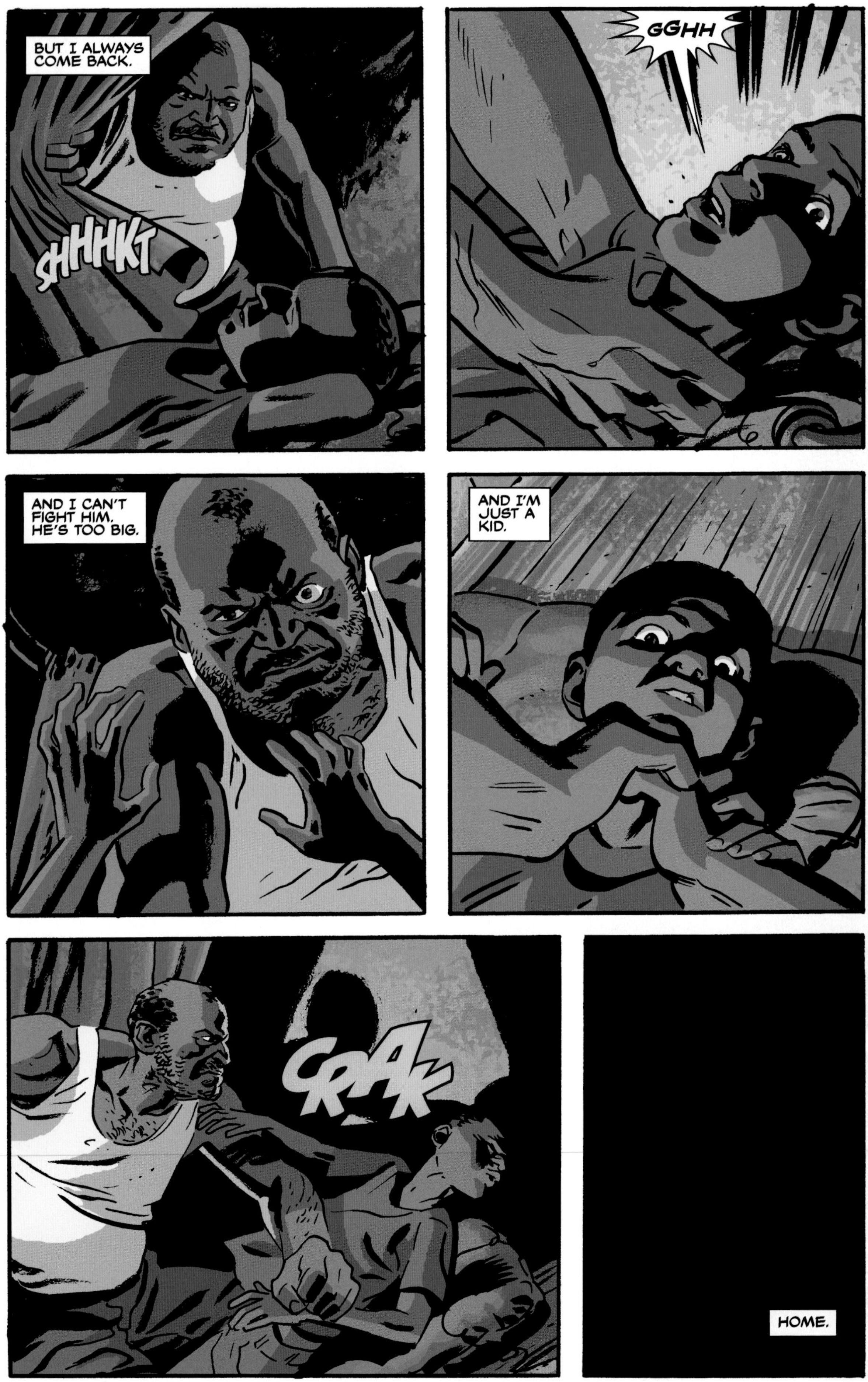
BUT I ALWAYS COME BACK.
SHHHKT
GGHH
AND I CAN'T FIGHT HIM. HE'S TOO BIG.
AND I'M JUST A KID.
CRAK
HOME.

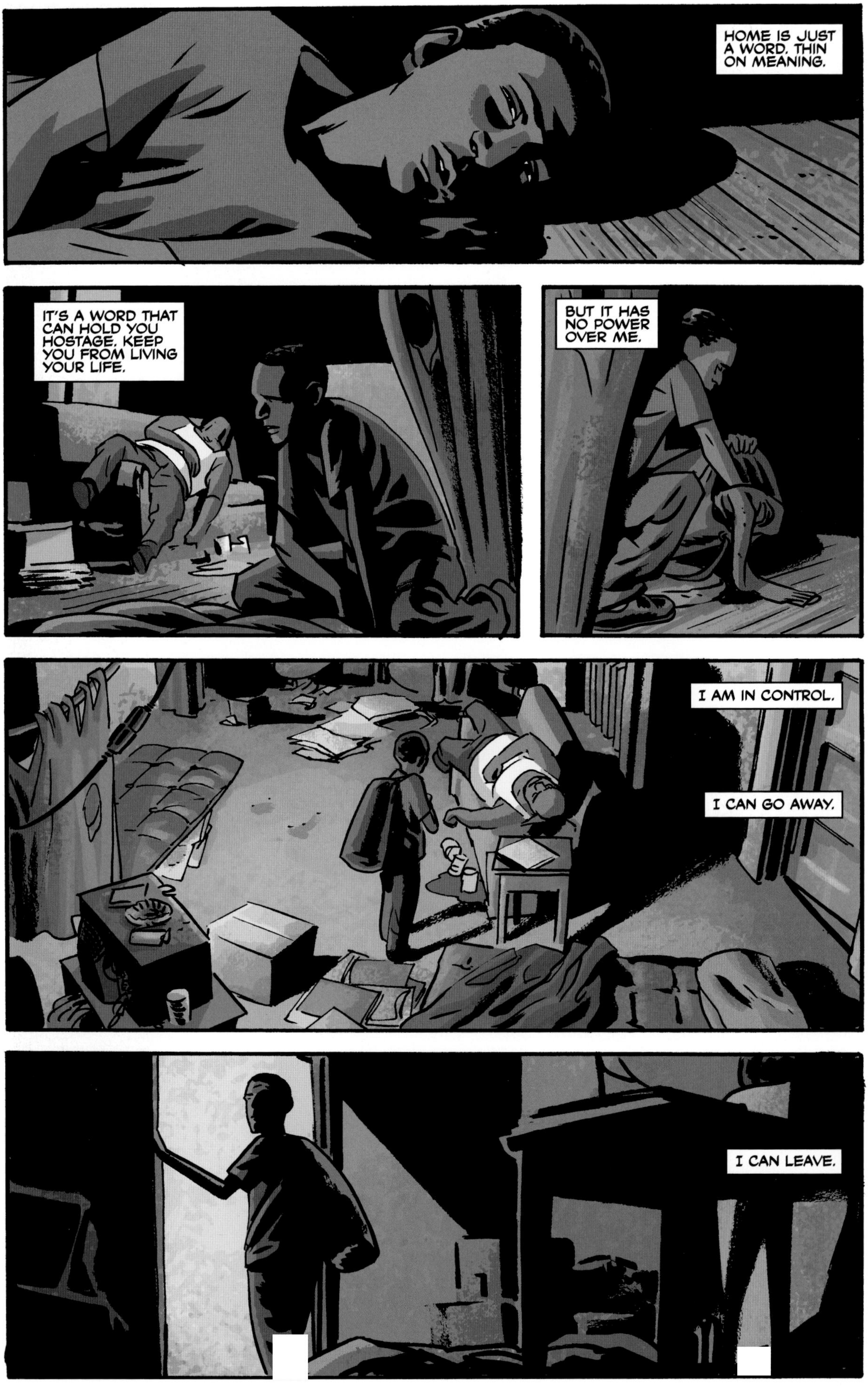
HOME IS JUST A WORD, THIN ON MEANING.
IT'S A WORD THAT CAN HOLD YOU HOSTAGE, KEEP YOU FROM LIVING YOUR LIFE.
BUT IT HAS NO POWER OVER ME.
I AM IN CONTROL.
I CAN GO AWAY.
I CAN LEAVE.

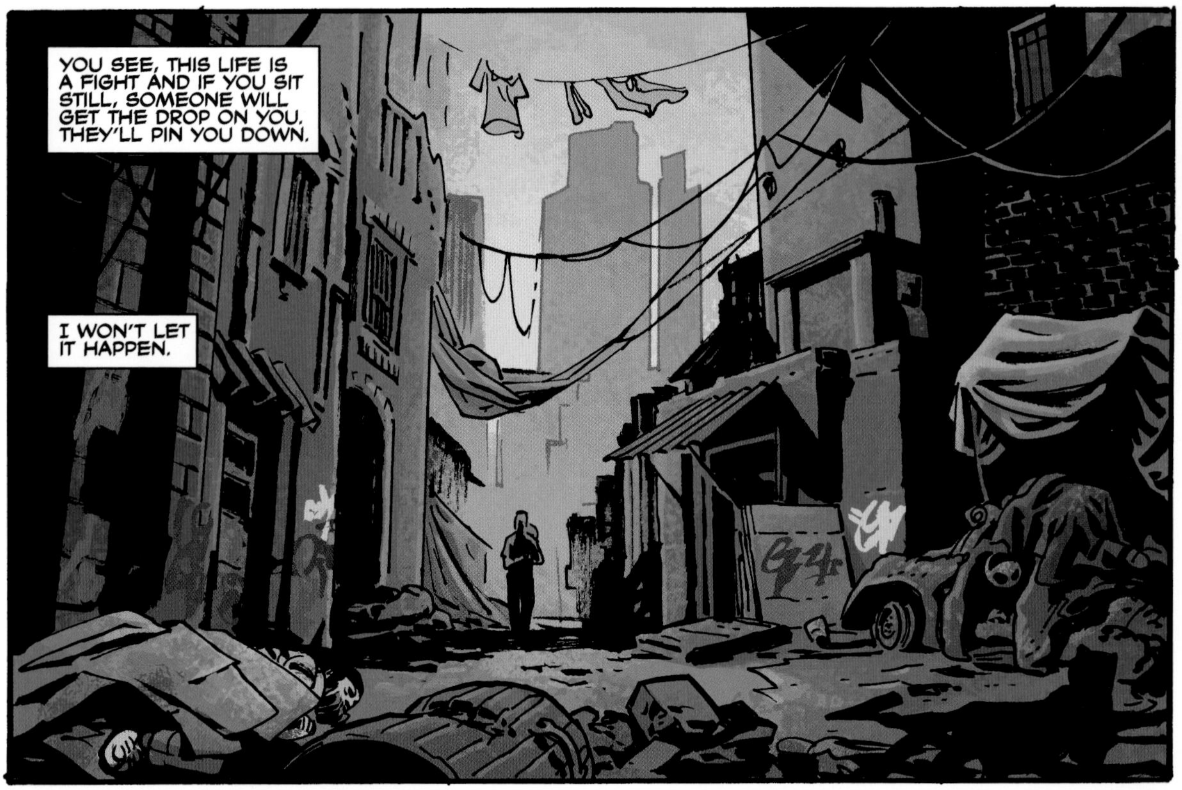
YOU SEE, THIS LIFE IS A FIGHT AND IF YOU SIT STILL, SOMEONE WILL GET THE DROP ON YOU. THEY'LL PIN YOU DOWN.
I WON'T LET IT HAPPEN.

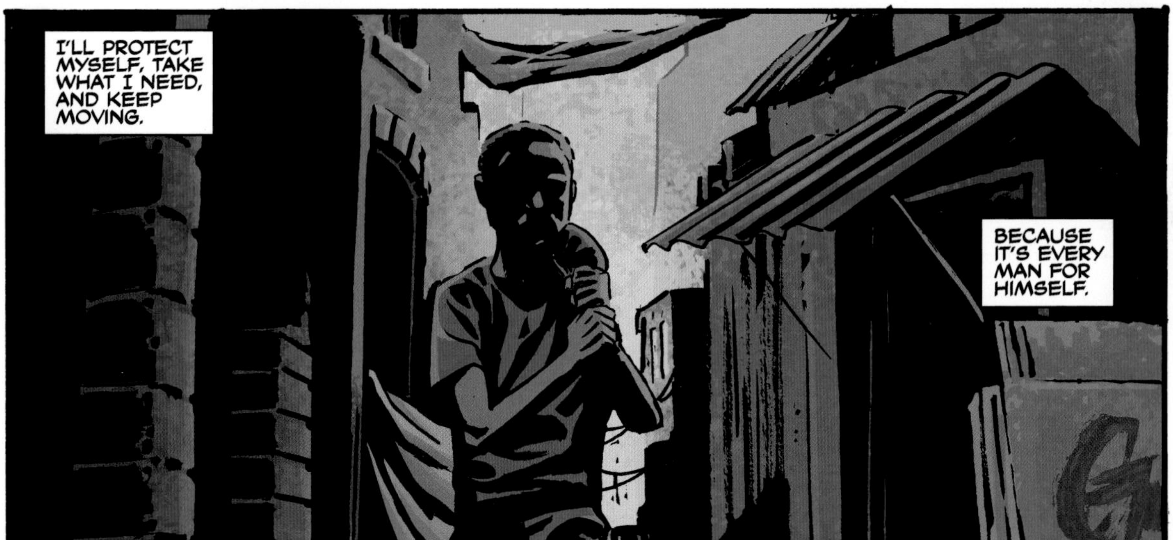
I'LL PROTECT MYSELF, TAKE WHAT I NEED, AND KEEP MOVING.
BECAUSE IT'S EVERY MAN FOR HIMSELF.

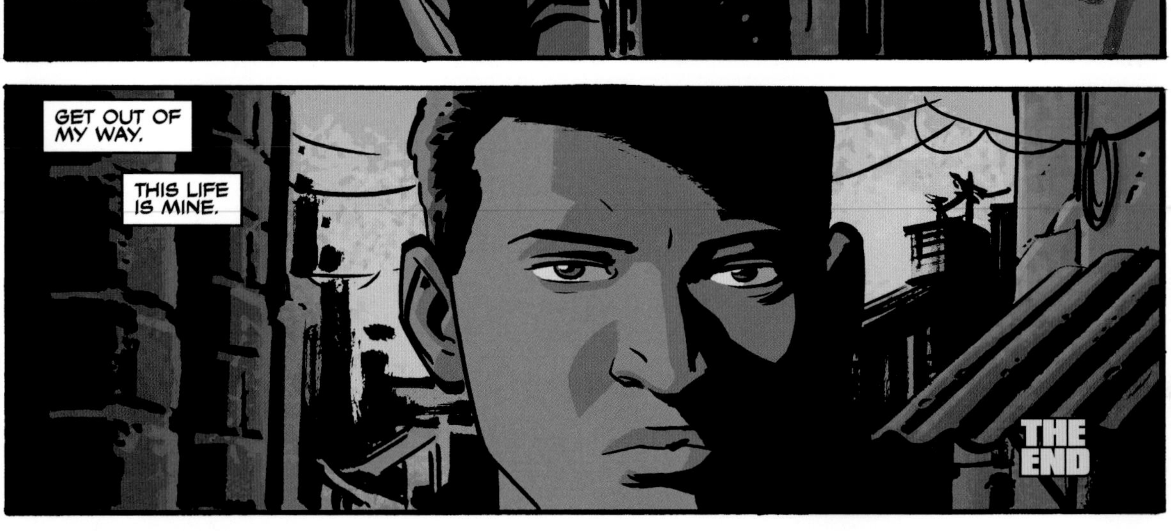
GET OUT OF MY WAY.
THIS LIFE IS MINE.
THE END

"THE JOURNEY IS THE WORTHIER PART . . ."

Now that I've been done with *The Shepherd's Tale* for eight minutes, I think it's a good time to reflect back on the experience with the clarity that hindsight provides . . .

I am a huge fan of the *Firefly* world, so it was a very exciting opportunity to be able to write something for it. It was fun too. I could write Jayne scenes all day long.

Most of all, though, it was nerve-racking. I didn't want to blow it. This is a beloved character from a beloved show, and I was about to tell his ultramysterious backstory. There are an awful lot of Browncoats out there, and they are a vocal bunch. It was important to me that I do the character justice.

I wrote the book, from an outline by Joss, in fits and starts between deadlines for other work. Luckily for everyone involved, the story lent itself to that method of writing, as every six pages or so it would change gears completely.

As I got deeper into Book's past I found inspiration in odd places. ESPN's documentary *No Crossover: The Trial of Allen Iverson* was a particularly unlikely source. When you watch that movie, you can see Iverson changed by the trial. He begins as a gifted, trusting, wide-eyed kid, and by the end of the process you can see he no longer has much faith in anyone but himself. He's on his own. There is something very lonely about the state that he ends up in, and I thought that was exactly where Book lived much of his life, believing that in this world it's every man for himself.

If you are curious to know where I got the idea for Book's abusive home life, you should listen to *Hast Thou Considered the Tetrapod?* by The Mountain Goats. It's sort of a direct steal. Sorry, Mountain Goats.

The last thing I wrote was also the most difficult. It was Book's narration over his death and over

his departure at the conclusion of the comic. Even though I'd spent a long time (I would tell you how long, but it's embarrassing) writing this story and thinking about this character, I was having a lot of trouble applying this finishing touch. I was tinkering with his death narration when I landed on a few lines that reminded me of one of Book's early encounters with Kaylee, when she asks him why he doesn't care what their destination is, and he replies, "Because the journey is the worthier part."

It struck me that Book is defined through and by movement. It's one of the reasons he fits in so well with the merry band of nomads aboard *Serenity*. It is a philosophy and a strategy. Keep moving.

As a young man Book mistakes movement for progress and runs away from things. He runs from abuse, imprisonment, and himself. He bounces around the 'Verse like a pinball. There isn't a tremendous amount of intent behind it beyond self-preservation. Hovering over a bowl of soup, there is a shift inside him, and his journey changes from one defined by what he is running from to one defined by what he is chasing: from self-preservation to self-discovery.

In remembering that moment from *Firefly*, I was able to uncover what the narration that ends the Book book should be. It's the journey that matters.

I have enjoyed my brief time in the 'Verse and hope that I've honored the amazing character Ron Glass created in the show. Chris Samnee obviously did an incredible job on his end. I was continually blown away by his work, as I'm sure you were.

Thank you for reading. It's been fun.

—Zack

FROM JOSS WHEDON

BUFFY THE VAMPIRE SLAYER SEASON 8:

VOLUME 1: THE LONG WAY HOME
Joss Whedon and Georges Jeanty
ISBN 978-1-59307-822-5 | $15.99

VOLUME 2: NO FUTURE FOR YOU
Brian K. Vaughan, Georges Jeanty, and Joss Whedon
ISBN 978-1-59307-963-5 | $15.99

VOLUME 3: WOLVES AT THE GATE
Drew Goddard, Georges Jeanty, and Joss Whedon
ISBN 978-1-59582-165-2 | $15.99

VOLUME 4: TIME OF YOUR LIFE
Joss Whedon, Jeph Loeb, Georges Jeanty, and others
ISBN 978-1-59582-310-6 | $15.99

VOLUME 5: PREDATORS AND PREY
Joss Whedon, Jane Espenson, Cliff Richards, Georges Jeanty, and others
ISBN 978-1-59582-342-7 | $15.99

VOLUME 6: RETREAT
Joss Whedon, Jane Espenson, Cliff Richards, Georges Jeanty, and others
ISBN 978-1-59582-415-8 | $15.99

VOLUME 7: TWILIGHT
Joss Whedon, Brad Meltzer, and Georges Jeanty
ISBN 978-1-59582-558-2 | $16.99

TALES OF THE SLAYERS
Joss Whedon, Amber Benson, Gene Colan, P. Craig Russell, Tim Sale, and others
ISBN 978-1-56971-605-2 | $14.99

TALES OF THE VAMPIRES
Joss Whedon, Brett Matthews, Cameron Stewart, and others
ISBN 978-1-56971-749-3 | $15.99

FRAY: FUTURE SLAYER
Joss Whedon and Karl Moline
ISBN 978-1-56971-751-6 | $19.99

SERENITY VOLUME 1: THOSE LEFT BEHIND
Joss Whedon, Brett Matthews, and Will Conrad
ISBN 978-1-59307-449-4 | $9.99

SERENITY VOLUME 2: BETTER DAYS
ISBN 978-1-59582-162-1 | $9.99

SERENITY VOLUME 3: THE SHEPHERD'S TALE
ISBN 978-1-59582-561-2 | $14.99

ALSO FROM DARK HORSE . . .

BUFFY THE VAMPIRE SLAYER OMNIBUS

VOLUME 1
ISBN 978-1-59307-784-6 | $24.99

VOLUME 2
ISBN 978-1-59307-826-3 | $24.99

VOLUME 3
ISBN 978-1-59307-885-0 | $24.99

VOLUME 4
ISBN 978-1-59307-968-0 | $24.99

VOLUME 5
ISBN 978-1-59582-225-3 | $24.99

VOLUME 6
ISBN 978-1-59582-242-0 | $24.99

VOLUME 7
ISBN 978-1-59582-331-1 | $24.99

BUFFY THE VAMPIRE SLAYER: PANEL TO PANEL
ISBN 978-1-59307-836-2 | $19.99

MYSPACE DARK HORSE PRESENTS VOLUME 1
Featuring "Sugarshock" by Joss Whedon and Fábio Moon
ISBN 978-1-59307-998-7 | $17.99

Buffy the Vampire Slayer™

·GEORGE·
OWENS

DARK HORSE BOOKS®
darkhorse.com

AVAILABLE AT YOUR LOCAL COMICS SHOP OR BOOKSTORE!
To find a comics shop in your area, call 1-888-266-4226.
For more information or to order direct: • On the web: darkhorse.com • E-mail: mailorder@darkhorse.com • Phone: 1-800-862-0052
Mon.–Fri. 9 AM to 5 PM Pacific Time.
*Prices and availability subject to change without notice

"THE JOURNEY IS THE WORTHIER PART . . ."

Now that I've been done with *The Shepherd's Tale* for eight minutes, I think it's a good time to reflect back on the experience with the clarity that hindsight provides . . .

I am a huge fan of the *Firefly* world, so it was a very exciting opportunity to be able to write something for it. It was fun too. I could write Jayne scenes all day long.

Most of all, though, it was nerve-racking. I didn't want to blow it. This is a beloved character from a beloved show, and I was about to tell his ultramysterious backstory. There are an awful lot of Browncoats out there, and they are a vocal bunch. It was important to me that I do the character justice.

I wrote the book, from an outline by Joss, in fits and starts between deadlines for other work. Luckily for everyone involved, the story lent itself to that method of writing, as every six pages or so it would change gears completely.

As I got deeper into Book's past I found inspiration in odd places. ESPN's documentary *No Crossover: The Trial of Allen Iverson* was a particularly unlikely source. When you watch that movie, you can see Iverson changed by the trial. He begins as a gifted, trusting, wide-eyed kid, and by the end of the process you can see he no longer has much faith in anyone but himself. He's on his own. There is something very lonely about the state that he ends up in, and I thought that was exactly where Book lived much of his life, believing that in this world it's every man for himself.

If you are curious to know where I got the idea for Book's abusive home life, you should listen to *Hast Thou Considered the Tetrapod?* by The Mountain Goats. It's sort of a direct steal. Sorry, Mountain Goats.

The last thing I wrote was also the most difficult. It was Book's narration over his death and over his departure at the conclusion of the comic. Even though I'd spent a long time (I would tell you how long, but it's embarrassing) writing this story and thinking about this character, I was having a lot of trouble applying this finishing touch. I was tinkering with his death narration when I landed on a few lines that reminded me of one of Book's early encounters with Kaylee, when she asks him why he doesn't care what their destination is, and he replies, "Because the journey is the worthier part."

It struck me that Book is defined through and by movement. It's one of the reasons he fits in so well with the merry band of nomads aboard *Serenity*. It is a philosophy and a strategy. Keep moving.

As a young man Book mistakes movement for progress and runs away from things. He runs from abuse, imprisonment, and himself. He bounces around the 'Verse like a pinball. There isn't a tremendous amount of intent behind it beyond self-preservation. Hovering over a bowl of soup, there is a shift inside him, and his journey changes from one defined by what he is running from to one defined by what he is chasing: from self-preservation to self-discovery.

In remembering that moment from *Firefly*, I was able to uncover what the narration that ends the Book book should be. It's the journey that matters.

I have enjoyed my brief time in the 'Verse and hope that I've honored the amazing character Ron Glass created in the show. Chris Samnee obviously did an incredible job on his end. I was continually blown away by his work, as I'm sure you were.

Thank you for reading. It's been fun.

—Zack